Glovebox Guide

BIRDS OF BRITAIN

This book describes and illustrates well over 160 species of birds which can be seen at various times of the year and locations throughout Britain. The book has been designed as a practical spotter's guide. Identification hints are given for each bird — size, markings, calls, flight characteristics, distinctive habits and so on — together with details of where and when to look.

The introduction describes typical habitats and how birds fly, feed, reproduce and migrate. There are also helpful hints and advice on bird watching and, at the back of the book, details of many locations and reserves noted for their bird populations.

KT-557-259

About the authors

Nicholas Hammond has been Director of Information and Education at the Royal Society for the Protection of Birds since 1986, having joined the staff as editor of *Birds* in 1966. Born in London in 1943, he has had a life-long interest in birds and natural history and became a junior member of the RSPB in 1955. He has been closely involved with the development of RSPB literature, and has written and contributed to several books on wildlife. Recent work includes a book about 20th-century wildlife art. He is married with two daughters.

Rob Hume was born in Staffordshire and has been bird watching seriously since the age of 14. He studied geography at University College, Swansea, and in 1976 began field work in mid Wales for the RSPB. He moved to RSPB headquarters at the beginning of 1978 to work in the development department and became editor of *Bird Life*, the magazine of The Young Ornithologists' Club, in 1983. He has written and provided illustrations for several books on birds, and is a leader of bird-watching holiday tours.

ACKNOWLEDGEMENTS

The publishers gratefully acknowledge the following for the use of their photographs. The photographs from pages 7—17 were supplied by the Royal Society for the Protection of Birds, and taken by the following photographers (where more than one picture appears on a page, credits are listed top to bottom).

7. Jane Miller, John Reynolds, Fritz Pölking **8.** Both Ernest James **9.** S Porter, Robin Williams **10.** Barry Angell, Hansgeorg Arndt **11.** R Mills, John Markham **12.** P Crellin **13.** W Paton **14.** Dennis Green **15.** Hansgeorg Arndt, W Paton, David Sewell **16.** R Mills **17.** Dennis Green, D Doig **27.** Stephen Krasemann/Natural History Photographic Agency (goosander)

The remainder of the book's photographs were supplied by Nature Photographers Ltd, except in the following cases: **68.** Maurice Walker (marsh tit) **72.** Laurie Campbell/Natural History Photographic Agency (feral pigeon) **87.** Maurice Walker (greenfinch) **115.** Both AA Picture Library.

Glovebox Guide

BIRDS OF BRITAIN

Nicholas Hammond
and Rob Hume

Produced by the Publishing Division
of The Automobile Association

4

Editor: *Roger Thomas*
Art Editor: *Harry Williams FCSD*
Illustrations: *Andrew Hutchinson*
Cover photograph: *Gannets, AA Photolibrary*
Typesetting: *Afal, Cardiff*
Printing: *Purnell Book Production Ltd, a member of
        the BPCC Group*

Produced by the Publishing Division of
The Automobile Association

Distributed in the United Kingdom by the
Publishing Division of The Automobile
Association, Fanum House, Basingstoke,
Hampshire RG21 2EA

The contents of this publication are believed
correct at the time of printing. Nevertheless, the
Publishers cannot accept responsibility for errors
or omissions, nor for changes to details given.

ISBN 0 86145 681 5

Published by The Automobile Association

BIRDS OF BRITAIN

Contents

WHAT TO LOOK FOR

Of all the animals that live in the wild in the British Isles, birds are the easiest to see. This is because they fly, are relatively tolerant of human beings, are usually active during the day and are present throughout most of the year. If you think about it, mammals are rarely seen during the day, insects are most active in the summer, reptiles and amphibians (of which we sadly have very few in our islands) spend several months in hibernation, and fish hide themselves away underwater.

It is hard to think of anywhere in Britain where it is not possible to see wild birds every day of the year. In the middle of a city the only birds you will see might be feral pigeons, starlings or house sparrows, but observant people may notice a grey heron or a kestrel flying overhead. Exciting and unusual birds turn up in the most unexpected places. When you know what to look for and where to look, you will discover birds when you go on holiday, on trips to the country, on your way to work and in your own garden. It can be very exciting to see unfamiliar species, but much of the pleasure of bird watching comes from observing the activities of birds, even — perhaps especially — those you know well. This book is meant both as an aid to identification and as a guide to observing and understanding the behaviour of the birds you see.

BIRDS AS ANIMALS

The feature that makes birds different from other animals is not egg laying (fish and reptiles also do that) nor flight (bats, which are mammals, can fly). The feature birds share with no other class of animal is feathers. Feathers are remarkable. Not only are they an effective method of insulation from cold and heat, but they also provide an essential element in the ability birds have to fly. Feathers combine to make a plumage that also creates protective colouring or adornments used during the process of display to other birds.

Top and above: *Feathers can affect the appearance of a bird. The robin's feathers are fluffed up in the snow to conserve heat, while in summer the bird has a sleek, slim appearance*

At first glance a feather looks simple, but it is really a clever construction of slender barbs with tiny hooks which 'zip' together. The shape of the feathers varies with the use to which they are put. Flight feathers are stiff and firm, while down feathers are soft. It is vital that a bird keeps its plumage in the best possible condition. A plumage in which the feathers have become damaged soon becomes useless. For this reason birds spend a considerable time preening, and renew their feathers by moulting. Most species moult once a year, very often at the end of the breeding season, but some may do so more often. In ducks the moult occurs in the summer and the males lose their brightly coloured feathers to become more drab like the females: this has the effect of camouflaging the birds at a time when they are flightless (whilst their flight feathers are being renewed) and is known as 'eclipse'.

BUILT FOR FLIGHT

In order to fly, birds have to have very powerful wing muscles and light bones. One of the reasons that man-powered flight is so difficult to achieve is that the human muscles are just not strong enough to lift a person from the ground even if wings are attached to the arms. A bird can fly because it has a deep keel-shaped breastbone to which are anchored the muscles that operate the wings. Weight is important too and if the bones of birds were filled with marrow as are those of mammals, they would be too heavy. Instead they are hollow, strengthened by a honeycombed structure. The heaviest flying birds in Britain are the swans which weigh in at around 15kg.

Swans in flight

EGGS

An embryo developing in a bird's body would be a distinct disadvantage in flight. Birds' method of reproduction allows the embryo to develop outside the body — in the egg. Once mating has taken place, the egg develops and is laid very quickly. The egg needs warmth to develop. This is provided by the incubating bird's 'brood patches', areas of the underside from which it loses feathers and where the blood vessels are very close to the surface. These brood patches occur only among the sex that incubates. Gannets lack brood patches altogether because they use their webbed feet to regulate the warmth of their eggs.

The nest and eggs of a song thrush

Details of laying and incubation vary between different kinds of birds. Some birds begin incubation immediately after laying the first egg, which means that the last egg to be laid may hatch several days after the first. Others do not begin to incubate until the last egg has been laid.

The length of time that incubation takes also varies. In some small songbirds it is as little as 11 days, but it may be up to 80 days among large seabirds such as albatrosses. In many species the female alone incubates. In others, males take a share and in a few species it is the male which does all the incubation.

CHICKS

Some birds — the nidifugous species — are well developed when they hatch, emerging covered in down, able to walk and to see and capable of feeding themselves, though some chicks (specialist feeders, for example, such as snipe and oystercatcher) are fed by adults. Whatever the feeding method, these nidifugous species are still brooded by their parents for some days. Other birds still need to be fed for some days after hatching, and the familiar garden songbirds hatch naked, blind and helpless. They are termed nidicolous. They remain in the nest and grow rapidly over the next few weeks as they are fed and brooded by their parents. They fly instinctively but may often be coaxed from the nest by their parents.

Naked, nidicolous chicks are hatched from the song thrush's eggs

FLIGHT

Birds fly in different ways, depending on the way they live. Many woodland birds have an undulating flight, moving through the air in a series of gentle dips and climbs. As the bird climbs it loses speed, so it always flies up to a branch where it lands as it is slowing down. The kestrel, by contrast, is a bird of prey that lives in open country. It searches for its prey by hovering several metres from the ground, dropping like a stone on any unwary small mammal it spots beneath. To enable it to hover with its head into the wind it needs a tail that can be spread, and long wings, the tips of which can be quivered to hold its position. Compare this

A kestrel hovering in typical hunting pose

The swallow's long tail aids manoeuvrability

to the sparrowhawk, a similarly sized bird of prey, which feeds on small birds in woods and hedgerows. The sparrowhawk catches its prey on the wing, so it needs to be able to fly very quickly, snatching its prey in the confined space of a hedge or a tree. For this reason it has broad, round-ended 'fingered' wings and a long tail that gives it manoeuvrability.

An interesting difference can be seen between two common summer visitors that share similar habitats. The swallow and the house martin are closely related and both nest on buildings, feeding on insects which they catch in their mouths in midair. Both have the narrow pointed wings ideal for swift flight, but the house martin has a short tail while the swallow's is long. This is explained by the fact that the house martin usually feeds on flying insects at least 6m from the ground while the swallow swoops low scooping flies as close as a metre to the surface. The swallow's feeding habits require it to be highly manoeuvrable to avoid obstacles such as bushes, cattle or cricketers! Large animals, be they cows or people, disturb insects from the grass, which is why swallows are often seen skimming pastures or even country cricket fields. The nesting habits of the swallow also require manoeuvrability because the bird tends to nest in relatively enclosed spaces such as barns and porches, while the house martin nests higher but in more accessible places under the eaves of buildings.

Some larger seabirds that spend much of their lives on the wing over the sea, searching for food, have developed so as to fly with the minimum of effort for as long as possible. They use the fact that windspeed is slower near the surface and faster between 12 and 24m above the sea. Gannets use the fastest part of the wind to build up speed, then glide down at a shallow angle on their long narrow wings, and then, wheeling, soar up against the wind, ready for the next downward sweep.

Look carefully at the shape of birds' wings. Are they rounded, fingered, pointed or square ended? Are they long or short? Are the wing-beats deep or shallow? How regular are the wing-beats? Are the wing-beats interspersed with glides? When the bird is gliding, how are the wings held? Are they bowed, straight or curved upwards?

The way in which a bird lands may also give a clue to its identification. Most ducks, for example, land on water with their wings held back and the webbed feet stretched out as brakes against the water, but the long-tailed duck glides down and lands on the water belly first.

MOVEMENT ON WATER

Gulls are generally very buoyant, with tails and heads held high. Some ducks, such as goldeneyes and eiders, swim low in the water with heads slumped into their shoulders, unless they are moving forward very quickly. Some species dive beneath the surface frequently. This is mainly associated with feeding, but may also happen where the bird is disturbed. Little grebes, for example, sometimes seem to disappear completely when they dive, but in reality they emerge from the water out of sight in the cover of vegetation.

MOVEMENT ON LAND

The way a bird moves on land can also help you identify it. The skulking behaviour of the very common dunnock means that it is frequently overlooked, but it is this behaviour that makes it easy to identify: a small, grey-brown blur seen among the shrubs in the garden will probably be a dunnock. In winter it is easy to distinguish between the fieldfares and redwings feeding in a field because the fieldfares hold themselves in much more upright positions. On the seashore,

A sanderling running (left) and a longer-beaked dunlin

sanderlings, small pale-grey waders, are easily identifiable because of their rapid movements, like little clockwork toys.

FEEDING

Much of a bird's life is taken up with the very important activity of feeding. In order to exploit all the opportunities for food, different species have become specialised in finding particular foods in particular places. Several species which appear to be feeding together may each be exploiting a different source of food. This can be seen quite clearly among waterbirds if you go to a gravel pit in winter. At the water's edge there might be a heron, standing motionless and waiting to strike at fish with its long sharp bill. On the water there will almost certainly be mallards, the least specialised of all the ducks, capable of feeding on the water by up-ending and

A male mallard up-ending in search of food. Note the curly tail feathers, unique to the male of the species

The motionless grey heron, waiting for a passing fish

taking underwater plants, or by pecking at floating seeds, as well as having the ability to walk on their longish legs and graze nearby fields. The closely related shoveler has a huge spoon-shaped bill which it moves across the surface filtering water through a comb-like arrangement within the bill which holds seeds and other floating food. Further out there might be tufted ducks, diving ducks capable of staying underwater for up to 24 seconds and normally diving to a depth of about 3m (though they have been recorded diving much deeper) in search of snails and other small aquatic animals. Another diving waterbird is the coot, whose near relative the moorhen is much more likely to be feeding near the water's edge or in nearby fields. Finally you will probably see the mute swan, whose long neck enables it to search further beneath the surface than other birds.

The shape of a bird's bill is an excellent clue to the way in which it feeds. Among the small birds that can be seen in parks and gardens, those that are predominantly seed eaters have thick bills that crack open the seeds. Finches are a good example. The shape of the bill varies from the very stout bill of the hawfinch, strong enough to crack a cherry stone, to the relatively slender bill of the goldfinch, which probes thistle heads for seeds.

The greenfinch has a powerful, seed-cracking bill

Those with slim, pointed bills are predominantly insect eaters. These birds, like the wren, use their fine bills to probe amongst crevices for insects. Blackbirds and song thrushes, whose diet includes larger insects, worms, berries and seeds, have heavier bills which are still pointed enough to probe amongst the soil in search of earthworms.

The curlew has a long bill which it uses in its search for worms

Birds with hooked bills are usually carnivores: the bills are ideal for tearing at flesh. Birds of prey and owls have talons with which they catch and hold their prey. Much of the bone, fur and feathers in their prey is indigestible and is regurgitated as pellets. Many other species also cast up pellets of undigested material — waders' pellets contain pieces of shell, and rook pellets often contain corn husks.

Wading birds have long legs to enable them to feed in shallow water and long bills with which to probe the mud for shellfish and worms. Turnstones have shortish bills with which they really do turn over stones in search of shrimps and other small animals, while the oystercatcher uses its hefty bill to prise open mussels.

Some birds, often the most successful ones, have not specialised. Starlings, for example, will feed on a great range of foods, particularly those provided by man, and are therefore found throughout the British Isles. Several other species have learned to exploit people. House sparrows and gulls are typical.

Swallows now build their nests exclusively on buildings. So do most house martins, although a few still nest on cliffs.

HABITATS

As well as food, birds need cover in which to roost and to nest. Some species will breed in one habitat: the bittern, for example, will only live in reedmarsh. Other species, such as carrion crow, may be found in every habitat from mountains to mud flats, because they are highly adaptable and are capable of eating almost anything.

Very few places in the British Isles have not been affected by human influence. This has not necessarily been a bad thing for birds, which make good use of 'created' habitats such as buildings, reservoirs, hedges and pastures, to name only a few. But some types of natural habitats have suffered and now need to be protected if the species that rely on them are to survive: much of Britain's reedmarsh, for instance, is now found in nature reserves.

The habitats of Britain can be divided into several main types. It is possible to sub-divide them further, although this is more relevant to the study of animals such as insects whose survival may well depend on a single plant species.

The main habitat types to be found in the British Isles today are:

○ *Sea*
○ *Seashore (as distinct from the following three coastal habitats)*
○ *Estuaries and mud flats*
○ *Sea cliffs and rocky islands*
○ *Saltmarshes*
○ *Slow-running rivers*
○ *Freshwater marshes*
○ *Lakes, ponds and reservoirs*
○ *Wet meadows*
○ *Arable farmland*
○ *Downland*
○ *Gardens, parkland and orchards*

Guillemots breed on sea cliffs

- Urban land
- Scrub and hedges
- Heathland
- Coniferous woodland
- Native pine forest
- Broadleaved woodland
- Moorland
- Fast-running streams
- High mountain

Because birds can fly they may stray from their normal habitats, especially after storms when they may be blown off course, or in very severe cold spells when they may move away in search of food. Whenever there are really cold winters there are reports of strange birds being seen in unexpected places.

BIRD MOVEMENTS AND MIGRATION

Birds also move to different areas in the normal course of events as they search for food. Everyone knows that swallows spend the winter in southern Africa, but it is not generally realised that most other birds move in search of food and very few spend all the year in the same place.

In the Arctic Circle conditions are inhospitable to the great majority of birds for most of the year, but in the short Arctic summer conditions are good enough for several species to breed. As the weather becomes worse in autumn, they move south. With its milder climate and plentiful food around the coasts and estuaries, Britain is a wonderful wintering refuge for the waders and wildfowl that breed in the wastes of the far north.

However, even in our country winter conditions are not suitable everywhere for birds. Few birds can survive the winter on the high tops of the Highlands of Scotland. The ptarmigan, a species of grouse, can tolerate the snow and, indeed, moults into white plumage, but many moorland birds move down from the uplands to sheltered valleys.

Other species like the cuckoo may breed in scrub or hedgerows in summer but migrate to Africa for the winter. Because they lay their eggs in other birds' nests, cuckoos do not need to stay to raise the chicks, and begin to return south in July, much earlier than most birds. The young cuckoos migrate south in August and early September, unaccompanied by any adults. Swallows and cuckoos are labelled summer visitors because none remain throughout the winter. With other species such as the blackcap, some stay and some fly south, so they are described as summer migrants and residents. Many species that we think of as resident, such as robins and woodpigeons, are joined in winter by more robins and woodpigeons from northern Europe. Other species are described as passage migrants because they stop in the British Isles on passage to and from their breeding grounds further north and wintering areas further south.

Birds migrate in order to find food. In very hard winters British birds and birds wintering here from elsewhere will move south in search of food, often crossing the Channel and Irish Sea. The brent geese that winter on the Channel coasts move between England and France at will.

The availability of food affects the numbers of birds. When food is plentiful, more young will survive, and some birds will lay more eggs when food is readily available. This breeding success may fluctuate from year to year, as with owls, and from place to place. For example, a pair of great tits nesting in a garden will rear fewer young than a pair nesting in a nearby deciduous woodland, because in woods there are thousands of caterpillars while the garden pair have to search more intensively for smaller insects.

Waders such as redshanks, curlews and turnstones are migrating birds

HOW BIRDS ARE GROUPED

In the previous pages we have seen just how varied birds can be. Taxonomists (biologists who classify the natural world) divide them into large groups or orders. All the ducks, geese and swans are members of one order while all the perching birds are members of another, even larger order. The main divisions within an order are the 'families', within which are smaller groups (or *genera*) of very closely related birds. The smallest sub-division is the species. A species is a group of birds of one 'kind' or 'type' that is able to breed and produce young that will be able to reproduce. Sometimes species may interbreed but these hybrids, or cross-breeds, like mules, are infertile.

Swans are members of an order that includes ducks and geese

Top: *The hooded crow of the far north of Britain is of the same species as — though different in appearance to — the carrion crow*
Above: *A male blackbird, with its albino mate*

Hybrids seem to occur most frequently among ducks and the odd hybrid in a flock of wild ducks will keep many bird watchers guessing. Sometimes members of the same species may show different characteristics in different geographical zones. The carrion crow, found in southern Britain, is replaced by the grey and black hooded crow in the north of Scotland. Where the two races overlap they interbreed successfully.

The birds in this book are arranged so that closely related species are grouped together. The most primitive species are at the beginning of the book and the most highly developed are at the end. We begin with grebes, cormorants and heron, and progress through ducks and geese, birds of prey, waders, gulls and so on.

WATCHING AND IDENTIFYING

Like any other form of identification, recognising birds is to some extent a process of elimination. As you learn more about birds you will find that this process becomes very quick. At a distance it is often not possible to identify a bird's species, but you can put it into its correct group. Long legs, a long neck and a long, thin bill mean that a bird is a wader. As it gets closer you may be able to eliminate some species because of the way it moves. You may even be able to identify the bird without being close enough to see its colouring or plumage pattern. The long curved-down bill of the curlew and its large size compared with other waders, together with its distinctive call, make it easy to identify even in silhouette against the sun.

Birds are very often seen in silhouette, or in some other way that makes them quite unlike the illustrations in books. It is therefore good practice to become familiar with the birds you see frequently. For example, you will learn to identify a blackbird at a distance because of its habit of cocking its tail on landing. Characteristics like this are known by dedicated bird watchers as 'jizz', a combination of the way a bird looks and moves. Bird watchers learn to recognise the 'jizz' of birds much as it is possible to recognise friends at a distance by the way in which they hold themselves and move.

Look at the way in which birds fly and get into the habit of distinguishing different sorts of flight. Woodpeckers have a dipping flight. Snipe will zigzag. Herons are slow and ponderous. Waders have rapid wing-beats and some species often fly in close, wheeling flocks.

Spot the difference. The black-tailed (left) and the bar-tailed godwits are closely related waders. The white on the wing of the black-tailed identifies it, while the bill of the bar-tailed is more upturned and the legs are shorter

Plumage colours and patterns are an obvious aid to identification but remember that the light may affect the colours you see. In the evening sun a house sparrow may look golden orange. Colour can also actually prevent birds from being seen because they are camouflaged. The woodcock, which nests among dead leaves on the ground in woods, has colours and patterns that help it to merge into the background. The wheatear, on the other hand, has bold markings, but in its rocky moorland breeding habitat can be very difficult to see because its colouring is disruptive, breaking up the bird's outline and effectively camouflaging it against the background of rocks.

The three redwings in this photograph can be distinguished from the fieldfare in the foreground by the pale lines over their eyes

The wheatear blends in well against a rocky background

Particular features to look for are the rump and tail patterns, because when we see birds they are often flying away from us. Many birds have wing bars which make identification easier. The shape of tails and wings are also features to look for. Although the colours of the fulmar and the herring gull are broadly similar, their wing and body shapes are quite different. Fulmars have narrower, straighter wings and a shorter body.

Finally, there are a few points to remember in looking at birds. Birds have a very keen sense of hearing and good eyesight. Do not move suddenly or make sudden noises. Use cover whenever possible. Cars make extremely good hides, even though they may be brightly coloured. You are much more likely to see birds by sitting quietly in one place and waiting for the birds to come to you, than by tramping around and disturbing them.

The information in this book is arranged to give an idea of how the bird looks. The measurement given is the length of the bird from bill to tail, but because judging size is so difficult, some comparison with other birds is often given. Unless stated otherwise, the sexes are alike. Behaviour, where it is a good clue, is briefly described. Calls are described phonetically. Distribution, food and habitat are also mentioned both as background information and as clues to identity.

Captions: please note
When there is a significant difference in appearance between the male and female of a species, the captions to the photographs/illustrations in the remainder of this book will specify the sex of the subject.

BIRDS OF BRITAIN

GREAT CRESTED GREBE

Podiceps cristatus 48cm

A long neck, pointed bill and ornate face frills make the great crested grebe in spring and summer quite unlike any other swimming bird in Britain. It is slightly smaller and much less bulky than the mallard. In autumn great crested grebes moult and the face frills disappear until next spring, but the pointed bill, slender neck and gleaming white breast are features that remain distinctive.

The feathers of this bird were used by Victorians to make 'grebe fur' muffs and by the turn of the century grebes were very rare indeed. Now, thanks to better protection and an increase in suitable habitat, they can be seen in most parts of the country. Gravel pits, reservoirs, shallow lakes and broad rivers are the best places to look for this spectacular bird.

The sexes look similar and they perform elaborate courtship displays in spring. Their nests are large untidy heaps of floating weeds anchored to bankside plants. Grebes spend almost all their lives on or under the water. They feed mainly on small fish and aquatic insects, which they catch by diving from the surface and submerging for up to half a minute.

Great crested grebe

LITTLE GREBE

Tachybaptus ruficollis 27cm

Even smaller than the moorhen, the little grebe or dabchick is much less obvious than the great crested grebe. During the breeding season this dumpy little bird is found on most types of slow-moving or still water where there are marginal waterside plants in which to build its nest of weeds, heaped until they are just above the surface of the water. Breeding normally begins in April and up to six eggs are laid.

Little grebe

In summer adults of both sexes are dark brown with chestnut throats, neck and cheeks, and the base of the bill is a noticeable yellow. In autumn the bill becomes completely dark and the chestnut plumage gives way to pale brown. The call is a loud, rapid trill, almost like a high-pitched neigh, often heard before the bird is seen.

They are shy birds, sticking, in the breeding season particularly, to the cover of aquatic plants. Little grebes are practically never seen on dry land. The main food of dabchicks is small fish and other water animals such as insects and snails, which they find by diving. Although the average length of a dive is only 15 seconds, little grebes sometimes seem to disappear totally, because they often come to the surface in the cover of plants after the dive.

GANNET *Sula bassana 95cm*

A magnificent, large white seabird with black wing tips, the adult gannet is unmistakable. In flight its body is cigar shaped and the wings are very long. Seen at close range the head of the adult is a strong golden buff. Immature gannets are dark brown speckled with white, taking four years to reach full adult plumage. As a bird reaches maturity more white appears in the plumage and immature birds look like piebald adults.

Gannets breed mainly on rocky offshore islands around northern and western coasts. Bass Rock in the Firth of Forth and Bempton Cliffs in north Humberside are the two most easily reached colonies. Outside the breeding season immature birds move south to the Atlantic off western Africa, but many adults stay in British waters.

A flock of fishing gannets is a spectacular sight, as these snow-white birds plunge from as much as 30m above the surface of the sea. As they hit the water a plume of white spray rises into the air, almost as if the bird has bounced off the sea.

FULMAR *Fulmarus glacialis 48cm*

This grey and white seabird looks like a gull at first glance, but its wings are straight and narrow, its body is rather solid and its tail is grey. The fulmar flies strongly, with bursts of wing-beats followed by glides on outstretched wings, or soars on up-draughts along cliff faces or over waves, like a small albatross. It has external nostrils along the top of its yellow bill, with salt-secreting nasal glands.

The fulmar is a marine bird that lives mainly on fish and carrion taken from the surface of the sea. Nevertheless there are breeding colonies in Edinburgh and Kinross several miles from the sea. Nesting

Fulmar in flight and head detail

is normally on sea cliffs, but in some places nests may be found along tumble-down walls.

While the majority of fulmars spend most of the year at sea, some may be seen throughout the year around our coasts, returning to coastal waters in November; breeding birds are back at their colonies in the spring.

MANX SHEARWATER
Puffinus puffinus 35cm

This remarkable bird lives over the ocean all year round except when it needs to nest. Then it comes to land, only under cover of darkness. Most colonies are on Welsh and Scottish islands. It is black above, silky white below, and may be seen offshore, flying low over the sea in a series of looping glides with short bursts of quick, stiff wing-beats.

RED-THROATED DIVER
Gavia stellata 58cm

This slender bird has legs set so far back that it cannot stand, and breeds very close to the edge of the Scottish lochs. In winter it is more widespread around the coasts of Britain, but then it loses the grey head and dark-red throat patch of summer to become a grey-brown bird with white speckles above, and a white face, throat and breast.

CORMORANT

Phalacrocorax carbo 90cm

Standing with its wings outstretched on a breakwater, the cormorant looks a heraldic bird. Its white cheeks and throat and white patch on the thigh make this large black bird easy to distinguish in summer from the more slender, smaller shag. However, outside the breeding season, the plumage becomes duller and the white side patch disappears. Even so, the cormorant can still be distinguished because it is bulkier, with a heavy bill which it carries with a distinctive upward tilt when swimming.

The juvenile cormorant has a dull-yellow face, dull-white underparts and dark-brown neck, wings, beak and tail. Cormorants eat fish which they catch by diving from the surface and swimming underwater. Although mainly maritime, cormorants visit inland waters in increasing numbers outside the breeding season. There is a nesting colony at Bird Rock near Tywyn in mid Wales, more than 7 miles from the sea. They breed in colonies around Britain's coasts except for the south and east between the Isle of Wight and Humberside.

SHAG *Phalacrocorax aristotelis 73cm*

Like the closely related cormorant, the shag has a somewhat prehistoric look, but in its breeding plumage it is a really splendid bird. Its black plumage has an oily green iridescence with a prominent forward-facing crest and its thin bill has a noticeable yellow gape. In winter the plumage loses its gloss and both crest and yellow gape disappear.

Shags are smaller than cormorants; white is absent from the face and they have much more slender bills and abrupt foreheads. In flight (usually low over the sea) the wing-beats are faster and are sometimes interspersed with glides. When it dives the shag makes a distinct jump out of the water before submerging. It catches fish to a depth of 4m, usually diving for about half a minute and using its large webbed feet to swim beneath the water. Although shags are more common than cormorants in the British Isles, most of them breed in Scotland and their habit of breeding on sheltered, undisturbed cliff ledges and sea caves makes them less widely known.

Shag

GREY HERON *Ardea cinerea 94cm*

Its large size, long legs and long, heavy bill make the grey heron very difficult to confuse with any other British species. The overall impression is of a big grey and white bird. The grey wings have black tips,

Grey heron

and black and white shoulder patches are particularly obvious when the bird is standing. In the breeding season the bill changes from yellowish-green to reddish-yellow. You can recognise immature birds because they are uniformly grey and lack the black markings of the adults on the head and neck.

A flying heron looks ponderous with its broad wings beating slowly, but it is in fact a strong and steady flier. The neck is drawn back, producing a noticeable bulge and the legs extend beyond the tail with the long toes clearly visible. The call is a harsh, loud 'pranck' or 'kraak'.

When it fishes, the bird stands motionless at the water's edge, poised to strike with its large, dagger-like bill. After it swallows a fish the heron will invariably wash its bill. Although fish make up the bulk of the heron's diet, other food

includes small mammals, insects, frogs, worms and other birds. The heron may be seen searching for this food some distance from water.

In severe winters the British population may be almost halved and it may take up to seven years for numbers to recover. The normal British breeding population is around 5,000 pairs, which nest at colonies of up to 200 birds. The nests are huge structures of twigs and branches built high in trees. Sometimes smaller birds like sparrows will take up tenancy in the twigs at the base of the heron's nest.

BITTERN *Botaurus stellaris 75cm*

Bitterns are rare in the British Isles, with less than 30 breeding pairs, and it is largely thanks to conservationists that they survive at all. The RSPB's reserves at Minsmere and Leighton Moss are places at which visitors have a good chance of seeing these interesting birds.

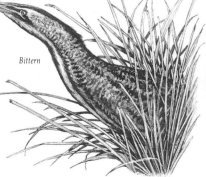

Bittern

Although related to the grey heron, the bittern's black-streaked golden and buff plumage and less lanky build make it look very different. In flight the broad wings give it a rather owl-like appearance, but its large green feet protrude noticeably beyond its tail. The bittern's famous booming call is made in April and May.

MALLARD *Anas platyrhynchos 58cm*
The mallard, our commonest duck, is found throughout the British Isles. The male has a bottle-green head, white collar and chocolate breast and the rest of the body is largely grey and brown. When the wing is outstretched during preening or flight, there is a purplish-blue panel (the 'speculum') on the wings.

open ground to holes in trees. The average clutch size is 12 and the young emerge covered in down and able to feed themselves. They stay in the nest less than a day, but are cared for by the female, which broods them at night until they

Mallard (female)

grow too large. Some mallards nest as far as 2 miles from water and the mother leads the ducklings to water when they leave the nest. Ducklings are easy prey for foxes, cats and other predators, but the female will draw predators away from the young by pretending to be wounded.

During eclipse from late July to September the male loses his bright plumage and takes on a duller hue, similar to the female, which is smaller and drabber but still has a purplish-blue speculum. Look carefully and you will see that the eclipse males retain vestiges of their normal plumage pattern.

All domestic varieties of ducks, except the muscovy, are derived from the mallard. This means that mallards will successfully interbreed with domesticated ducks. As a result, some very strange-looking ducks can be seen on town ponds. Although males and females form pairs in autumn and stay together throughout the winter, it is the female which incubates the eggs and rears the young. Indeed, the pair bond breaks down during incubation and the male mallard subsequently has nothing to do with his offspring.

Like many successful species, the mallard is broad minded in its choice of nest sites, which may be anything from

GADWALL *Anas strepera 50cm*
Slightly smaller than the mallard, the gadwall is not nearly so common. At a distance both sexes seem grey, although the male's black rear is noticeable; both have a white speculum. The male has a brown head, grey breast and back and white belly. It is found on fairly shallow, standing or slowly moving waters.

Gadwall (male)

TEAL *Anas crecca 36cm*

Smaller than any other British breeding duck, the teal is scarcely bigger than a moorhen. The drake is a splendid creature with a dark chestnut head and a broad, metallic-green eye stripe fringed by a thin cream stripe. The chest is cream coloured blotched with large spots, and there is a cream patch edged with black beneath the tail. The female is speckled brown and has a noticeably white line along the middle of the wing in flight. Both sexes have a green and black speculum.

The teal's habit of springing into flight almost vertically has given rise to the collective noun 'spring' being used to describe a group of the birds. Their calls are rather wader-like: the males have a double whistle and females a sharp, high 'queek'. This small duck is found in a variety of habitats from pools and bogs in uplands to estuaries and saltmarshes.

Wigeon

patches in front of the tail. In flight the wings show distinctive white patches at the front. The female is rusty-brown, sometimes greyer, with a clean white belly and a short, blue bill. Flocks graze on turf near reservoirs, on flooded meadows and over saltmarshes, often steadily advancing in a tight group.

Most wigeon come from Iceland and northern Europe from September to March, but a few hundred pairs breed in northern moors near small pools.

PINTAIL *Anas acuta 57cm*

The slim, graceful male pintail does indeed have a long, pointed tail but his gleaming white breast, and a line of white extending up from each side of the neck into the dark brown of the head, are much more easily seen. Females are rather pale brown, with grey beaks. Pintails are winter visitors, found on many estuaries and some lakes, but only in a few places, such as the Mersey, are they at all common.

Teal (male)

WIGEON *Anas penelope 49cm*

Winter flocks of this medium-sized duck are very lively, colourful and noisy gatherings. Wigeons are neat, short-necked, small-billed ducks, with very short legs and short but pointed tails. The male has a red-brown head, set off by a primrose-yellow forehead, a pink breast, silver-grey body with a horizontal line of white each side and black and white

Pintail (male)

SHOVELER *Anas clypeata 48cm*

Swimming low in the water and feeding with its huge spoon-shaped bill, the shoveler looks rather squat. The male's bright golden eye contrasts with its green-glossed black head, which with chestnut underparts, white breast and black stern combine to make a spendidly coloured duck. The female is speckled brown with the same large bill. Both sexes have pale grey-blue forewings which are eye-catching in flight.

Shoveler (male)

Shelduck (male)

British shovelers breed in lowland areas, moving south in winter, so that many of the birds seen here in winter come from Iceland and Northern Europe. Shovelers avoid coastal waters, except briefly on passage, preferring shallow lakes, gravel pits with shallow margins and marshes. They feed around the edges of lakes, using a series of bristles inside the bill to filter floating plant and animal matter from the water.

SHELDUCK *Tadorna tadorna 63cm*

Shelducks bring startling flashes of colour to estuaries. Both males and females have black heads (on rare occasions with a green gloss), white bodies with a broad chestnut band, and black patches on their backs. The males have black bellies and a pronounced knob at the base of the extraordinarily vivid red bill. The tips and trailing edges of the wings look very dark from a distance, giving the impression of a black and white bird in flight. The wing-beats are slower than those of other ducks but faster than those of geese.

Juveniles are duller than their parents, but have the characteristic shelduck shape. The head and back are grey-brown and the underside pale grey. The ducklings' dark-brown and pale-grey plumage give them a pied appearance.

In the British Isles shelducks are largely shorebirds, preferring muddy coasts and estuaries and feeding on small snails and shellfish. They often breed some distance from the shore among sand dunes, meadows and woods, in rabbit burrows and holes in trees. They have large families, a pair raising 5—11 young. Soon after hatching the family moves to a new feeding ground and remains together for up to three weeks or until the adults succumb to the urge to migrate across the North Sea to the German Waddensee where most European shelducks gather to moult. The young form into creches of up to 100 birds under the charge of a few remaining adults.

Manx shearwater

Red-throated diver

Gannet

Cormorant

Mallard (male) in winter

Teal (male)

Wigeon (male)

Pochard (male)

Tufted duck (male)

Long-tailed duck (male)

Eider (female)

Goosander (male)

Red-breasted merganser (male)

Greylag goose

Canada goose

Whooper swan

Bewick's swan

Mute swan

TUFTED DUCK *Aythya fuligula 44cm*

The black and white male tufted duck is common on inland waters, such as reservoirs, gravel pits and park lakes. It is rather small and rounded, as buoyant as a cork, frequently disappearing underwater as it searches for tiny aquatic animals. The male has a wispy crest hanging from the

Tufted duck (male)

back of the head. Females have a trace of the tuft; they look simply all dark brown, unless they fly when broad white wing bars show up well.

In flight tufted ducks are fast, despite the chunky shape, and if disturbed, by a boat perhaps, often rise high from a lake only to circle round and drop down again on the other side.

POCHARD *Aythya ferina 46cm*

The pochard is marginally larger than the tufted duck, with which it is often seen in winter, and its sloping forehead contrasts with the tufted's steeper profile. The male appears to be tricoloured with its chestnut head, black breast and tail, and pale-grey back and sides. A pale-grey bar can be seen running the length of the wing when the bird flies. The female has a less striking pattern in shades of brown but there are distinctly lighter marks around the bill and the eyes, giving a frosty look to the face.

The pochard is not a common breeding bird here, but birds from north-west Europe and Russia settle in large flocks on reservoirs and gravel pits, moving to coastal waters only when the winter becomes very hard. It is often possible to identify pochards at a distance, because they give a little leap out of the water before diving to find food. Their food, which is largely plant matter, is usually found between 1 and 2½m deep; they feed mostly at night and spend much of the daytime sleeping.

GOLDENEYE *Bucephala clangula 47cm*

The goldeneye's triangular head, humped back and often cocked tail give it a distinctive shape on the water. At any distance most look very dark — actually grey, with darker-brown heads — and only the adult males (always a minority) stand out. They are brilliant white with black markings, with a white patch near the bill on an otherwise black head. The birds are frequent on larger lakes and estuaries in the winter months.

Goldeneye (male)

LONG-TAILED DUCK

Clangula hyemalis 45cm

Small flocks of this compact little duck, active and quick to take flight, appear in winter in the shallow seas of the north and east coasts. Males are largely black and white, with brown patches on the head and a long, flexible tail point. Females and youngsters are duller, with blackish crowns and white faces marked with a smudge of brown. They all have small, chunky heads and very short bills. They dive endlessly, except in spring when the males court the females, often giving loud, musical calls.

COMMON SCOTER

Melanitta nigra 48cm

The male scoter is all black except for a patch of orange on its bill. The female is dark brown with the lower half of the head dull white. They are usually seen in late summer or winter, far offshore, in buoyant flocks riding the waves, or flying low, just below the horizon, in long wavering lines close to the surface of the sea.

EIDER *Somateria mollissima 60cm*

Bulkiness is the most obvious quality of the eider, which is large and has a long triangular head and stout bill. Males are black underneath, white on top and marked with lime-green patches on the nape. They have a strong pink colour on the pale breast. The female shares the male's bulky shape but is brown, mottled above and neatly barred beneath. The birds fly rather heavily, low over the surface and swim well with heads usually sunk into the shoulders, but spend much of their time loafing out of the water gathered in small groups.

Eiders are coastal birds, breeding north from Northumbria in the east and Ulster and Cumbria in the west, moving southward a little in winter. Their nests are lined with down, used for centuries by man for quilting, and in Britain and Iceland this has resulted in a long history of protection.

Common scoter (male)

GOOSANDER *Mergus merganser 62cm*

The long thin bill of the goosander has a series of sawtooth-like serrations to hold the fish that it catches. It is a large duck, longer and bulkier than the mallard. The male's black head, long red bill, black back and pale-pink underparts make it unmistakable. The female, however, is easily confused with the female red-breasted merganser. Both females have shaggy chestnut heads, but the goosander

Goosander (female)

is larger and the demarcation between the chestnut of the head, the white chin and the pale-grey back is much better defined. The merganser is browner-grey, its pattern more blurred.

The goosander breeds in Scotland, northern England and Wales near lakes and rivers with mature trees which have holes in which to nest. Because the female spends much time away from the nest fishing, she lines the nest with wood chips and feathers to keep the eggs warm. In winter the birds are widespread on lakes and reservoirs. Goosanders feed almost exclusively on fish, which are caught by diving from the surface and staying underwater for up to two minutes.

RED-BREASTED MERGANSER
Mergus serrator 55cm

The red-breasted merganser is a 'saw-billed' duck, smaller and slimmer than the goosander. The spiky crest on the male's green-black head contrast with the smooth head of the goosander and it has a distinctive streaky ginger breast, broad white collar and grey sides. In flight it looks slender and fast, though not particularly agile.

The female has a chestnut head, but her crest is shaggier, her body browner and chin patch less well defined than that of the cleaner-looking male goosander. In flight both sexes show large squares of white on the wings.

Red-breasted mergansers swim rather low in the water and dive frequently to catch fish which are securely held by the serrated beak. Unlike goosanders they nest on the ground, in tall grasses or

Red-breasted merganser (male)

amongst bushes. The female covers the 8 or 10 eggs with down when she leaves the nest. By late summer families gather on the coasts of Wales and northern Britain where they nest and in winter immigrants from Iceland and northern Europe swell the population, these winter visitors reaching further south.

WHITE-FRONTED GOOSE
Anser albifrons 72cm

The white-fronted goose is one of the three 'grey' geese most commonly seen in the British Isles. At first glance all three look very similar, and it can be difficult to sort them out. The 'white front' refers not to its breast, which is notable for its ragged black bars, but to the white area aound its bill. This goose has a square-looking head, though in flight the dark markings on the breast are the best distinguishing feature. Its wings seem slimmer than those of other grey geese and it is a more agile flier.

Two races of the white-fronted goose spend winter in the British Isles. The Russian race has a rose-pink bill and prefers wet meadows. There are usually wintering flocks at the Wildfowl Trust's refuge at Slimbridge, and also on the north Kent marshes and in Norfolk. The Greenland race has an orange bill and winters on peat bogs in Scotland, Ireland and, in very small numbers, in Wales.

GREYLAG GOOSE *Anser anser 83cm*

The greylag is a large, pale-brown goose with a heavy build, thick neck, hefty orange bill and pink legs. Some birds have dark markings on the breast, but these are never as well defined as those of the white-fronted. Greylags fly with slower wing-beats than other grey geese and call with a deep, three-syllable cackle. The very pale forewing shows clearly from above and below.

On land the greylag has a much more rolling gait than the other grey geese and it walks very like a domestic goose. Indeed, all domestic varieties except the Chinese goose derive from the greylag. Greylags graze on land, preferring the fresh green parts of plants in summer and the roots and tubers in winter. In the water they take aquatic plants.

In Scotland there is a small natural breeding population. Although greylags ceased to breed in England in the first half of the last century, they were reintroduced in the 1960s and 1970s and now breed across the country wherever there is suitable water. The British breeding birds do not migrate, but other populations do and in winter Icelandic greylags visit the British Isles. These begin to arrive in large flocks in Scotland in the second half of October and leave in March or April.

White-fronted goose

BRENT GOOSE *Branta bernicla 59cm*

This is the smallest of the geese seen in Britain and Ireland. It is about the same size as a mallard, but can be distinguished from ducks by the white chevron on its tail and its much slower, bulkier appearance in flight. Head, neck, breast and back are all matt black and adults have white markings on the neck just below the head. The dark-brown wings with the black head and neck give flying birds a very dark appearance.

Brent geese

The colour of the underparts of the brents depends on their origin. Russian birds have dark-brown bellies, while the much scarcer brents from Greenland, Arctic Canada and the island of Spitsbergen have pale bellies.

Dark-bellied brents winter on estuaries and mud flats along east and south coasts. The light-bellied race winters in Iceland and in small numbers on the Northumbrian coasts. Flocks begin to arrive in October, but numbers are at their peak from December to February. They begin to leave in early March and have gone by mid-April.

Brent geese eat a wide range of plants, but a particularly important source of food is a marine plant called eel grass. They also feed in the water by taking plants from the surface and by up-ending.

PINK-FOOTED GOOSE
Anser brachyrhynchus 68cm

Smaller than either the greylag or white-front, the pink-footed goose is also much more delicate looking than either. The head, which is darker than the rest of the body, is small and the bill and neck are comparatively short. The legs are pink and the bill is black and pink. In flight the underwings show up dark and the wing-beats are fast and fluid, giving the goose an aerobatic appearance. Much of the romance that is attached to wild geese must be due to the pinkfoot being so vocal, making high-pitched calls and a three-syllable cackle.

Pinkfeet are highly gregarious migrants and winter in large and spectacular flocks. There may be up to 90,000 birds arriving in October and staying until April. Most winter in

Pink-footed goose

Scotland, but in England they can be seen in Lancashire, Humberside and around the Wash, while in Ireland there is a wintering flock in County Wexford.

Vegetarians, pinkfeet feed on stubble (being particularly fond of barley and oats) and potatoes. They feed during the day, flying to roost at night on mud flats or lochs, making an incomparable sight against an evening sky.

BARNACLE GOOSE
Branta leucopis 64cm

The barnacle goose is an immaculate grey and black bird. The head, neck, upper breast and rump are black, the face is creamy white, the underside very pale and the wings barred black and grey. There is a white crescent on the rump and the underside of the wings are pale, contrasting with the dark head and back in flight. Flocks fly in loose untidy formations. On the ground frequent quarrels break out among individuals and the flight call is a dog-like yelping.

In autumn they fly from the Arctic to the Hebrides, Ireland and the west coast of Scotland. They rarely associate with other species of geese, arriving in flocks at the end of September and leaving in the second half of May.

CANADA GOOSE
Branta canadensis 95cm

This is the largest British goose and it has a long neck, bulky body and very large feet. Like the smaller barnacle goose it has a black head and neck but its body is largely brown and the head is marked by a white 'chinstrap'. The tail is black and

Canada goose

there is a broad white chevron across the rump. Canada geese fly fast with strong measured wing-beats, often in V-shaped flocks, calling with a resounding honking. On the ground they walk rather sedately and they are excellent swimmers.

As its name suggests the Canada goose is not a native of this country. It is a North American bird, first introduced here for purely ornamental puposes in the 17th century. It is now common in urban parks and lowland areas where there is suitable water. It feeds in flocks in the water and on pasture and arable land, where it can become a pest.

The nest, a low pile of leaves, grasses and reeds built on the ground, is usually near water. About six eggs are laid and the young hatch covered in yellowish down and able to feed themselves, but they are cared for by both parents. Although they can fly at about six weeks they stay with their parents until the following spring, becoming fully independent at the start of the next breeding season.

Barnacle goose

MUTE SWAN *Cygnus olor 150cm*

The mute swan is the largest British bird and, being all white, one of the most easily recognisable. Adults have orange bills with a black knob at the base; immatures have grey bills and are smudged with brown. Mute swans are common on lakes, park ponds and rivers. After a long run to get airborne, they fly strongly, with a loud throbbing hum from the wings. The mute swan is not so silent as its name suggests, though its voice is restricted to a variety of hisses and strangled guttural noises.

WHOOPER SWAN
Cygnus cygnus 150cm

As large as a mute swan, the whooper looks slimmer and has a straighter, slender neck. It has a low forehead and this flattened look is increased by a large triangle of yellow on the bill. The call is a bugle-like clanging.

Whoopers are winter visitors to Britain (particularly Scotland) and Ireland. Almost entirely vegetarian, they feed on aquatic plants (found by up-ending or dipping the head beneath the surface) and grain, grass and vegetables found on land.

Mute swans

This swan will nest near almost any area of water with sufficient width for take-off. The large nest is a heap of reeds and other plant material gathered from the water nearby, and the eggs are huge and pale green. They are often the target of schoolboy egg thieves, but a protective swan is not to be taken lightly. Young swans are downy grey, their first feathers brown and patchy, but they become white within a year. When still very young they may hitch a ride on the back of a parent, usually the female. Eventually they are driven off and have to find a suitable territory of their own.

BEWICK'S SWAN
Cygnus columbianus 120cm

Differentiating between Bewick's and whooper swans can be difficult. They are rarely seen together, when size is the obvious difference, but the Bewick's can often be seen with the much larger mute swan. The Bewick's has a thicker neck than the whooper and less yellow on its bill. Bewick's swans also fly with strong, fast wing-beats and are noisier than whoopers, having a musical babble of shorter, less trumpeting notes.

Breeding in the Arctic Russian tundra, they visit Britain in winter. The best places to see Bewick's are Slimbridge in Gloucestershire and the Ouse Washes in Cambridgeshire from December to February. They feed on plant matter.

GOLDEN EAGLE *Aquila chrysaetos 80cm; wingspan up to 220cm*

Golden eagles are rarely seen by people who are not looking out for them, and even keen bird watchers may have to be content with a very distant view of a 'speck in the sky' high over a Scottish peak. The eagle is very large and can be seen with binoculars literally miles away, and its steady soaring at high altitude is a good pointer to its identity — a bird on a roadside pole will be a buzzard! It is much bigger than a buzzard or raven, with very

BUZZARD *Buteo buteo 54cm*

Buzzards are common in the south-west of England, Wales, the Lake District and much of Scotland, especially where there is an attractive mixture of open hills, wooded slopes and farmed valleys. They are smaller than eagles but bigger than a crow; they look mottled brown with creamy patches under the wings and fly with their wings raised in a slight V. Buzzards soar for long periods, though they will also hunt by sitting on a post and watching for rabbits or smaller fry, such as moles, worms and beetles. They will often scavenge dead rabbits killed on roads and, where common, can frequently be seen at close range.

Golden eagle

long wings, a protruding head and a longer tail than a buzzard's; adults are dark brown, but young ones have bold patches of white on wings and tail.

One or two pairs nest in the Lake District and about 420 pairs in Scotland. They need remote, open country in which to hunt hares and grouse and where dead deer and sheep provide food in winter. Live lambs are rarely taken, though these majestic birds are capable of killing quite substantial prey.

The call of the buzzard is a loud, challenging, ringing note which echoes around a narrow valley but becomes a thin 'mew' at longer range. It is a sound rarely heard east of the Welsh Marches, because past persecution and continued illegal poisoning by unenlightened gamekeepers have restricted its range to the wilder areas of Britain.

SPARROWHAWK *Accipiter nisus 33cm*

Most female birds of prey are bigger than their mates but this is taken to extremes in the sparrowhawk; such a difference enables the females to eat larger prey, such as thrushes and pigeons, without competing with the males, which eat finches and tits. The male is a neat little hawk, long tailed but short winged, blue-grey on top and barred with orange beneath. The female is browner, with off-white underparts barred with brown.

Sparrowhawk (female)

Kestrels are often mistakenly called sparrowhawks, but the true sparrowhawk never hovers, has much shorter wings and is more secretive. It dashes through woods or along hedges, taking its prey — nearly always birds — by surprise.

The sparrowhawk is a woodland bird, liking deciduous and coniferous woods equally well, though it ventures out over moorland, open fields and saltmarshes in search of prey. It flies fast, with a distinctive series of several wing-beats alternating with short, level glides. It is sometimes so reckless in hunting that it hits wire fences or windows, or even enters gardens.

RED KITE *Milvus milvus 63cm*

The red kite was once common throughout Britain and a familiar scavenger in the streets of towns. It is now confined to the hills and woods of mid Wales, but thanks to the efforts of conservationists, particularly the Nature Conservancy Council and the RSPB, its population, although still small, is increasing. Kites nest, roost and rest in the oakwoods that clothe the hillsides and feed over the open sheepwalks and moorland. In winter they forage in lowland farm pastures and bogs.

Marginally larger than the buzzard, the red kite looks more slender and elegant in flight. The long, narrow wings are held at an angle and the long tail is forked, although this becomes less noticeable when the tail is spread. Overall, the colouring is a reddish-brown but the wing tips are black and the head whitish; in addition, there are large white patches under the wings.

Red kites fly with a deep, relaxed wing action. They soar with wings held forward, manoeuvring with ease, by gently angling either wing, tail or body. They feed on both carrion and live prey, which includes voles, moles, rabbits, birds and large insects.

Red kite

OSPREY *Pandion haliaetus 57cm*

As it plunges into water to take a fish in its feet, the osprey is one of our most spectacular and dramatic birds. It is still a very rare bird but many thousands of people each year watch ospreys at the RSPB observation point at Loch Garten, near the Cairngorms in Scotland. Our breeding ospreys all nest in Scotland and

Osprey

spend the winter in Africa. These and some Scandinavian ones can be seen in autumn and, more briefly, in spring, as they move over on migration, pausing at a large lake or reservoir to snatch a fish or two as they go.

Larger than a buzzard, the osprey is dark brown above, with a white head crossed by a black mask, and white beneath except for a brown breast band and black patches beneath the wings. The wings are characteristically held in a slight upward kink at the wrist with the tips drooped, giving a somewhat gull-like shape.

Ospreys have huge feet with spiky scales and very long, sharp claws, specially adapted to grasp slippery fish, usually pike, trout or flatfish from shallow estuaries. They nest on crags or ruins or, more usually nowadays, in the tops of tall pines, making a bulky structure of thick sticks which, despite its size, can be surprisingly hard to find.

MARSH HARRIER

Circus aeruginosus 52cm

The chocolate-brown female marsh harrier is as big as a buzzard, but with the typically long wings and tail of the harrier family and a neat cream cap. Buzzards are rarely seen over the east-coast reedbeds which the harriers inhabit, and the harriers have a characteristic way of flying low, with wings held up in a V, as they look for small birds and voles. The males are smaller with largely grey wings, tipped black, and grey tails.

Marsh harrier (male)

Marsh harriers are very rare birds, happily increasing slowly, mostly confined to East Anglia but showing welcome signs of spread. Their restriction to freshwater marshes with extensive reeds gives them little opportunity ever to become much commoner, however. Like other harriers, the male gives food to the female in spring in a spectacular aerial foot-to-foot pass.

HEN HARRIER *Circus cyaneus 48cm*

Moorland in summer, and low, flat pastures or coastal marshes in winter, are the places to look for the hen harrier. It needs essentially open ground, because it hunts by flying slowly, at low altitude, searching for voles, mice and small birds. A sudden twist or burst of acceleration shows that it has spotted something and a dive to the ground usually results in a successful catch.

Hen harrier (female)

Males look ghostly pale against a dark moor. They have contrasting black wing tips and a white rump and underside, but are mostly pale grey. Females are dark brown with a much more obvious band of white across the base of the tail. They are slim, long tailed and long winged and fly with leisurely wing-beats interspersed with glides — when the wings are raised in a V — though they are not travelling as slowly as they seem. A few pairs try to breed in Wales and northern England, but gamekeepers hate harriers for killing grouse chicks and very few are allowed to rear their young. Such persecution has shown signs of intensifying in recent years, though the birds manage to remain rather more frequent in Scotland.

PEREGRINE *Falco peregrinus 42cm*

A hunter which catches birds on the wing, the peregrine is a spectacular flier. It was highly prized in the days when falconry was widespread, and was used among other things for hunting the much larger heron. Its flight is powerful; slow and steady over long distances with frequent glides, but swift and agile when hunting. The hunting peregrine will soar high to watch for flying prey, which is taken in a powerful, steeply angled swoop at as much as 80—100mph.

Females are 15 per cent larger than the males and are about the same size as the rook. The peregrine is compact with broad but pointed wings and a relatively short, broad tail. The upperparts are blue-grey with faint barring on the back and a pale-grey rump. The breast and underwing are finely barred. Immature birds are brown and streaked, not barred. At all ages the head looks blackish.

In Britain and Ireland peregrines breed in the uplands and on sea cliffs. Their nesting sites have in some cases been used for centuries, and some of today's sites were recorded by falconers as far back as the Middle Ages.

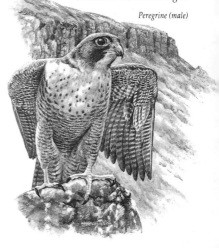

Peregrine (male)

KESTREL *Falco tinnunculus 34cm*

The commonest bird of prey in the British Isles with an estimated population of 100,000 pairs, the kestrel is found in every corner of Britain. Major roads with embankments and broad verges provide motorists with frequent sightings of kestrels hovering beside the carriageway in their search for small mammals.

The kestrel is a little larger than a mistle thrush, with longer wings and tail. The male, unusually for a falcon, is slightly larger than the female and more strongly patterned with grey head and tail, chestnut back and streaked buff underparts. The female is more uniformly brown with a barred back and tail. The bird's flight action is fairly fast with shallow wing-beats interspersed with glides, but it is the hovering, as if suspended on a string, that is so expertly done.

Small mammals, particularly voles, make up the bulk of its diet, but small birds are the main source of food for city-breeding kestrels. They seek out their prey by hovering, head to wind, up to 10m from the ground — the characteristic pose seen from motorways. Kestrels nest in a great variety of habitats on ledges and in holes in trees, in ruins and in specially made nest boxes.

Hobby in flight with house martins

HOBBY *Falco subbuteo 33cm*

Although it is about the same size as the much more common kestrel, the hobby has a shorter tail and longer, scythe-shaped wings. The shape of the wings and the hobby's fast flight make it look not unlike a large swift. The bird is strongly marked with a black head and striking white neck patches, dark blue-grey upperparts, streaked underparts and rufous thighs.

Hobbies catch high-flying birds, such as swifts and martins, and birds like larks and pipits that fly high when singing. Insects such as moths and dragonflies are caught in the foot and transferred directly

to the bill. The hobby then eats these insects whilst still in flight.

When it is hunting small birds it flies with a rather stiff wing action, with short glides between fast wing-beats, but when it is hunting flying insects it has more supple, relaxed wing-beats. It is a summer migrant which arrives in April and May and leaves in August and September. It breeds in the south of England and the southern Midlands, nesting in old crow nests in trees in areas of dry heath, downland, open woodland and mixed farming country.

RED GROUSE *Lagopus lagopus 40cm*

This round, rather dumpy gamebird is confined to heather moorland in the north and west of the British Isles. Its reddish-brown plumage, flecked with darker feathers like a fine heathery tweed, is excellent camouflage. At first glance the sexes look alike, but the male has a richer plumage and prominent red wattles on either side of his crown.

The wings are dark brown, square ended and rather short, and the bird has a dark, rounded tail that is very evident on take-off. Red grouse fly fast with bursts of rapid wing-beats interspersed with glides on down-curved wings. As it rises, a grouse calls with a sudden, cackling outburst like 'kok-kok-kok' then a repeated 'go-back'.

In Britain and Ireland the main food of the red grouse is heather, although some insects are eaten and form the bulk of the food of chicks. To provide the best conditions for grouse, the heather moors must be managed with regular burning to prevent the heather from becoming rank, and moors managed for shooting have the highest populations of red grouse. Males stake out territories in early autumn and pair with females with whom they stay until the young have been reared the following summer. Eggs are laid in April and early May.

PTARMIGAN *Lagopus mutus 35cm*

The rounded, densely feathered ptarmigan has a tough life on the very highest tops of the Scottish mountains and the far northern hills of Scotland where the terrain is equally harsh and barren at lower altitude. In most places it lives over 1,000m above sea level, where it feeds on bilberry and crowberry shoots and berries.

The ptarmigan is a little smaller than a red grouse and always has white wings, though they are practically hidden until it flies (and it is usually so remarkably tame that it prefers simply to walk away from people). In winter the plumage is entirely white, apart from the black tail; in spring it is blotched with brown and cream and in summer much greyer. Throughout the year it has the most appropriate camouflage for its surroundings.

Ptarmigan

Red grouse (female)

CAPERCAILLIE *Tetrao urogallus*
male 86cm; female 62cm

Capercaillies provide one of the most astonishing sights for bird watchers. When displaying to hold territory and attract a mate, the male swells his body, spreads his tail and distends his throat, leaping about a metre into the air at intervals and noisily flapping his wings.

The male capercaillie is a large, goose-sized woodland gamebird. Its overall plumage colour is dark grey and brown with some white under the tail and white shoulder spots. The roundness of the head is accentuated by a shaggy bearded throat. The female is only three-quarters the size of the male. Her plumage is delicately patterned with a rufous black-marked back, chestnut breast, paler underparts and a long, reddish, barred tail. The longish neck and rounded tail stick out in flight as the bird crashes out of a tree, or heather, at close range. The male has a raucous call like a man clearing his throat, whilst the female's sound is similar to that of a pheasant.

The capercaillie is a bird of Scotland's coniferous woodland, preferring well-grown forests with a good ground covering of bilberry. Plants form the main food and Scots pine provides food at all

stages — shoots, needles, seeds and cones are all consumed. The bird feeds mainly on the floor of the forest, moving up to the trees in winter.

BLACK GROUSE *Tetrao tetrix*
42cm; 14cm tail in male

Larger than the red grouse but smaller than the capercaillie, the male with his glossy blue-black plumage and lyre-shaped tail is unmistakable. There is a large powder puff of white under the tail and a white wing bar, most obvious in flight. The smaller female, which is warm brown and barred, has a gently forked tail and an obscure pale wing bar. The bird's flight is rapid with long glides on stiff, slightly bowed wings.

Black grouse in Britain are today confined to Scotland, the north of England, Wales and Exmoor. They are birds of the margins between woods and open country and may be seen in young conifer plantations. In the early hours throughout most of the year groups of up to 20 males will meet in 'leks' where they display to each other. In spring females visit the 'lek' to choose a mate, which after mating takes no part in rearing the young.

Black grouse (male)

GREY PARTRIDGE
Perdix perdix 30cm

Smaller and less bulky than the red-legged partridge, the grey partridge is much more subtly coloured with an orange face and grey underparts on which there is a large maroon horseshoe mark and reddish-brown marks on the flanks. It flies fast with several wing-beats interspersed with glides on bowed wings. It has reddish outer tail feathers similar to those of the

Grey partridge

red-legged partridge, but looks more streaked on the back. As it flies up the bird gives a sharp, rattling call; better known is the creaky, monotonous 'keerr-ik' given from a meadow.

The partridge is a ground-living bird of farmlands, found in cereal crops, meadows and pastures in eastern and southern Scotland, England, Wales and Ireland. Plants, including the green leaves of grasses, cereals, clovers, seeds and grain, are the bird's main food. The female makes a scrape nest which is lined with grass and leaves. She lays 10—20 olive-brown eggs and, while she alone incubates, her mate helps to care for the young and will brood them when they are small. Because they are ground-living birds, the eggs and young are vulnerable

to predators such as foxes, stoats and cats. The young are capable of flying at about a fortnight, when still only half grown. They stay with their parents until the early part of winter.

RED-LEGGED PARTRIDGE
Alectoris rufa 33cm

Large, heavily built but with a small, round head, the 'red-leg' is easily told from the grey partridge by its white face, outlined in black, plainer sandy-brown back and more boldly striped sides. It is harder to distinguish in flight, but prefers to run away from danger if it can.

It is a bird of open ground and is at home on the large cereal fields with light soils in the warmer, drier eastern counties of England; it is less happy and much scarcer in the west. The red-legged partridge feeds on seeds, leaves and roots,

Red-legged partridge

with a few insects to enliven its diet in summer. Unless disturbed it lives a quiet life, walking slowly and inconspicuously in pairs or family parties, but its loud, chuffing, 'steam-engine' calls are often very evident in spring.

PHEASANT *Phasianus colchicus*
male 77cm; female 60cm

The big, long-tailed, exotic-looking cock pheasant is at home in the British countryside and is common almost everywhere. Yet the pheasant is not a native British bird at all, and in many places only annual releases of captive-bred birds (for shooting) keep up the numbers. Its harsh 'kok-kok' call, followed by a sudden threshing of wings, is a frequent sound at dusk on the edge of a piece of woodland. Females are much less conspicuous, in a sober camouflage pattern of mottled brown.

A disturbed pheasant flies up in a heart-stopping clatter of wings but once airborne cannot go very far at such a speed and soon glides down to a sheltered spot. Pheasants nest on the ground in deep cover, with up to 15 eggs per nest. Males are often polygamous but take no part in incubating the eggs or rearing the young — hence the showy colours which are to impress mates but offer no real camouflage. All have dark-green heads and mottled brown bodies but the details vary; many have a white neck ring and paler rump, others are darker and more richly glossed chestnut.

WATER RAIL *Rallus aquaticus 26cm*

Because it is a skulking bird of reed beds and marshland, it is often easier to hear the water rail than to see it. The calls include a repertoire of squeals, grunts and whistles. Smaller and slighter than the moorhen, it has a long red bill, dark-brown back, dark-grey underparts with black and white striped flanks and pink legs. The sexes are alike.

Predominantly a feeder on creatures such as insects, spiders, amphibians and small fish, it will also eat seeds and plants. In very hard weather it will even feed around bird tables in riverside gardens. The water rail is both a resident and a winter visitor to Britain.

Water rail

Osprey

Buzzard

Peregrine

Kestrel (female)

Sparrowhawk (female)

Capercaillie (male in display)

Red grouse (female)

Pheasant (male)

Red-legged partridge

Lapwing (female)

Oystercatcher

Ringed plover

Golden plover

Woodcock

Green sandpiper

Bar-tailed godwit

Redshank

Greenshank

Sanderling

MOORHEN *Gallinula chloropus 33cm*
This common waterside bird is a frequent sight beside park lakes, slow rivers and even the smallest farm ponds. It swims with a to and fro bobbing action of the head and neck, and a pointed, cocked tail.

Moorhen

On land, where it often feeds on open grassy places, it has a nervous, twitching walk with head nodding and tail flicking constantly. It is a round-bodied, small-headed bird with huge feet. Its bill is brilliantly red, tipped with yellow, its back glossy brown and head and underside slaty-grey. Under the tail is an obvious white patch and a thin line of white curves over the flanks. Young birds have a similar pattern but are olive-brown on the dark parts and have a greenish bill.

Small chicks are endearing fluffy balls, all black except for their tiny red bills. Both parents share the work of incubating the eggs and feeding the chicks and, if a second or third brood is reared in a season, the older youngsters of the earlier broods will often feed the newest chicks. Family parties stay together during the winter, but flocks rarely exceed 20 or 30 birds, and moorhens are never seen in large numbers on open water as are coots, preferring a quieter, more sheltered life at the edge of the pool.

COOT *Fulica atra 37cm*
Larger and rounder than the moorhen, the coot is a dark charcoal all over except for its white bill and facial shield, and grey-green legs. On the water its rear end curves down, while that of the moorhen sticks up. The coot is much more at home in the water than on land.

The coot's food, mostly vegetable, is taken in a variety of ways — from the surface, by scraping algae from submerged stones, by breaking off aquatic plants, by up-ending, by feeding on land and by diving. Dives are short, lasting under 20 seconds and rarely exceeding more than 2m in depth.

Coots are very aggressive in defence of their territories during the breeding season. Fights between rivals are very noisy and there is a great deal of splashing. Both parents incubate and care for the young, which fly at about seven weeks. Chicks are covered in scruffy black down and have bald red heads. Their first covering of feathers gives them dark-grey upperparts and dull-white underparts. In the winter months, coots gather together in large numbers.

Coot

OYSTERCATCHER

Haematopus ostralegus 43cm

About the same size as a black-headed gull, the oystercatcher is a dazzling black and white wader with pink legs and a long, vivid orange-red bill. Adults in winter and juveniles have a white crescent around the throat. The call is a piercing 'kleep', often given in flight, and 'piping parties' of several birds stand together and call with an ear-splitting chorus.

Oystercatchers nest on rocky, sandy or pebbly seashore, saltmarshes and flat islets around the British coasts, but in Scotland and Cumbria they also nest inland on shingly river banks, lakesides and (Scotland only) arable fields. In winter they move to coastal mud flats and estuaries, where they form huge flocks, feeding on shellfish at low tide and moving to high-tide roosts amongst rocks or on saltmarshes.

LAPWING *Vanellus vanellus 30cm*

The lapwing is a striking bird with dark metallic-green wings and back and a long black crest. The breast is black, the underparts are white and a patch beneath the tail is orange. Its call is a strained 'pee-wee' which gives it the alternative name of peewit. In flight the lapwing has a most distinctive shape, with broadly rounded wings, and looks black and white.

In winter, large flocks feed in pasture and arable land on wireworms, beetles and other ground-living invertebrates. In spring the flocks break up and males begin to advertise their territories in lowland farmland (particularly wet meadows) and on upland moors. The display flight is an erratic tumbling and is very showy. The nest is a scrape on the ground in which four eggs are laid. Until fairly recently lapwings' eggs were collected to be sold as plovers' eggs in fashionable restaurants.

AVOCET *Recurvirostra avosetta 43cm*

With an upturned bill and startlingly white plumage marked with black, the avocet really is unmistakable. Because it is the symbol of the RSPB, the avocet is one of the best-known British breeding waders, even if it is one of the rarest. Avocets returned to breed in England in 1947. They have since spread from the reserves at Minsmere and Havergate to other sites in East Anglia and Kent. They are summer visitors to England and while most spend the winter in southern Europe and Africa, small flocks winter on estuaries in south-west Engand.

Avocet

RINGED PLOVER

Charadrius hiaticula 19cm

Sitting on its eggs on a beach, the ringed plover is well camouflaged with its sandy brown plumage and disruptive black and white face and breast markings. In spring and summer the legs are orange and the bill yellow with a black tip; in winter they are slightly duller.

Ringed plover

The bird is very active on the ground, running, pausing and tilting forward to pick up food, which consists largely of crustaceans, worms and molluscs. The ringed plover flies with very quick wing-beats, showing broad white wing bars and a dark-tipped tail with white outer tail feathers. The bird's call is a liquid, rising 'turwik'.

Most of the British and Irish breeding population breed on beaches around the coast where they are vulnerable to human disturbance. Nesting begins in April with the male making a shallow scrape. The normal clutch is 3—4 eggs, which, like the young when they hatch, are extremely well camouflaged among the sand and pebbles. Incubation takes 23—25 days and is by both sexes.

LITTLE RINGED PLOVER

Charadrius dubius 15cm

The little ringed plover is smaller and more delicate than the ringed plover. It also has a distinct yellow eye ring, a thin dark bill and less black on its head than the stockier ringed plover. Its legs are pink. When flying it has barely perceptible wing bars. The call is an abrupt, descending 'pew'. Little ringed plovers are summer migrants which begin to arrive in April and leave in September for Africa. Exposed gravel at pits provides the birds with excellent breeding conditions.

TURNSTONE *Arenaria interpres 23cm*

Turnstones really do turn over stones in search of food — small shellfish and crustaceans — on rocky coasts, shingle beaches and along the tangled, weedy strandline in sandy bays. Their short, stout, slightly upturned bills are ideal for the job.

Turnstones are rather small waders, with short, bright-orange legs. In winter they are swarthy brown and black except for white undersides and white patches in the wings which show as they fly. In spring they are transformed into very colourful birds with a tortoiseshell pattern of orange-ginger, black and white. They breed in Scandinavia and Greenland and move south in winter as far as southern Europe and Africa, passing through Britain in spring and autumn, but many stay all winter through.

Turnstone

GOLDEN PLOVER

Pluvialis apricaria 23cm

In winter a lapwing flock may be found to contain a mixture of smaller, less obvious birds which feed on the fields with a similar stop-start action, tilting forward to pick up worms and beetles in typical plover fashion. These are golden plovers, winter visitors to the lowland pastures from the high moors where they breed. In spring, before they return to the hills, they may be seen in glorious summer plumage, black beneath and on the face, and otherwise spangled with yellow, brown and black. Winter birds are much browner, pale beneath, but always spotted with yellow; their underwings are white.

In flight they separate out from the lapwings, flying faster on sharply pointed wings, calling with long, plaintive 'peeoo' notes. Similar sounds echo over the moors in summer, but the birds themselves are hard to spot as they stand motionless on a low rise, ever watchful and easily disturbed. Their nesting behaviour is complicated, with the best territories sometimes used by one pair early in the summer and another pair later on, taking full advantage of the opportunities in the richest sections of moor.

GREY PLOVER

Pluvialis squatarola 28cm

In summer plumage, all too rarely seen here, the grey plover is like a silver-grey-backed golden plover with some black below and a stripe of white along each side. In winter it becomes drab, pale grey with specklings of black. Its best feature shows up only in flight — then a black 'armpit' patch beneath the base of each wing makes it instantly identifiable. A white patch above the base of the tail is also unlike the uniformly dark-backed golden plover.

Grey plovers spend the winter on estuaries and large, undisturbed sandy beaches, where they walk about slowly, standing still for long periods in a dejected, hunched way. They have a long, three-note call, the middle one lower, like a boy whistling — 'whee-oo-ee'. In spring they leave for the far northern tundra in the Arctic, typical of so many globe-trotting waders which take advantage of the long hours of daylight and abundance of insects in the land of the midnight sun.

Grey plover in winter

SNIPE *Gallinago gallinago 26cm*

The days when thousands of snipe could be bagged in a day's shooting have long since gone, thanks largely to the drainage of almost all wet meadows and marshy places in lowland Britain. Today only 2,000 pairs nest in the lowlands and most snipe live in the higher moors of the north and west in summer, moving down in the winter months. They like nothing better than a sticky, muddy ooze with a patchy growth of rushes and tall grass, where they are safely hidden but able to search and probe for worms with their very long, straight bills.

WOODCOCK *Scolopax rusticola 34cm*

The woodcock is a mysterious and secretive inhabitant of dense, damp woodland, in which it is very difficult to find. Though the size of a large pigeon, its beautifully marbled and barred pattern of browns, black and buff makes it next to impossible to pick out from the dead leaf litter on the forest floor.

Woodcock

Snipe

Snipe are beautifully patterned, in browns, buff and black, with long pale stripes along their backs and stripy heads. They are not easy to see well on the ground, often rising suddenly with a sharp 'scaap' call, to zigzag high up into the air and fly far away. The dark wings with a light stripe along the trailing edge, long bill and short tail help to identify them.

In spring the male snipe advertises its nesting territory by flying high overhead, periodically diving down at an angle with its outer tail feathers stiffly spread. The bird vibrates in the air, making a humming, bleating sound, a performance known as 'drumming'.

Fortunately it has a distinctive territorial flight which allows us to see it quite easily in spring and summer, though only at dusk when little more than a stocky, broad-winged, short-tailed but very long-billed silhouette can be detected. Woodcocks fly low over the trees in apparently regular circuits, though the route can be changed from time to time and night to night. The bird flies steadily, with deep, slow wing-beats but a tremulous flickering of its wing tips. At the same time it utters a deep, double croak and a thin, sharp whistle in alternating sequence, a display known as 'roding'.

CURLEW *Numenius arquata 55cm*

In spring, moorlands and upland farms in the north and west ring to the song of the curlew, one of the most romantic of all bird sounds. The bird flies up, giving a series of long, melancholy whistling notes, then glides back to the ground, wings raised, while producing a beautiful, ecstatic bubbling trill. Its normal call gives it its name — a liquid, loud 'cur-lee'.

Curlew

Curlews are streaky-brown, long-legged and rather large birds, made distinctive only by the long and evenly downcurved bill. The female has a longer bill than the male. They probe into wet moss, boggy pools and, outside the breeding season, deep estuarine mud, and the bill is sensitive and flexible enough to detect then grasp hidden worms. It is also strong enough to deal with a fair-sized crab. In winter curlews are mostly coastal and feed in loose groups which have to gather together at undisturbed roost sites as the rising tide pushes them off the mud. Then they fly in long lines and Vs, looking rather gull-like, to rest in hunched, quiet groups until the receding waters allow them to spread out to feed once again.

They return to the moors and some lowland valleys in March and April. The nest is a mere scrape in the ground lined with grasses. The large eggs, olive mottled with brown, hatch after four weeks and it is another 5—6 weeks before the young are able to fly. Then the moors are deserted and quiet again until the following spring.

WHIMBREL *Numenius phaeopus 41cm*

Noticeably smaller than the curlew, the whimbrel has a comparatively shorter bill and a distinctive pale stripe bordered by two dark stripes on top of the head. It has faster wing-beats and when it feeds it probes more rapidly than the curlew. Its call is a very distinctive, rapid even trill.

The whimbrel is a very rare breeder in Britain, but is found in northern Scottish moors and islands. Its main breeding areas are the tundra of North

Whimbrel

America and northern Europe. It moves in winter to the African coast, mainly passing through the British Isles in April and May and from August to October, when it is usually seen on estuaries, mud flats and rocky coasts.

BLACK-TAILED GODWIT
Limosa limosa 42cm

After being absent from Britain as a breeding bird for over 100 years, the black-tailed godwit returned in the middle years of this century, irregularly at first, and is now a regular breeder at a few places, mostly in East Anglia. It is, though, still a rare bird.

unseasonal flooding and numbers are in decline. In winter the birds move to estuaries and are widespread but very patchy in their distribution, rarely mixed with bar-tailed godwits and nearly everywhere much scarcer.

Black-tailed godwit

It is a large, tall wader with an elegance of form that distinguishes it from its dumpier relative, the bar-tailed godwit. It has a longer, straighter bill and noticeably longer legs. In the breeding season it is a striking coppery-red on the breast and neck, white beneath and mottled brown above. In winter the lovely colours are replaced by sober greys. At any time, however, it looks spectacular in flight, with a broad white rump, black tail and black wings with a long, central stripe of white. Bar-tails are much plainer.

Black-tailed godwits breed in areas of low, damp moorland and blanket bogs in Europe, in Britain mostly in wet pasture in nature reserves. In early spring the splendid males fly high over their territories, rolling from side to side and making loud, lapwing-like calls. In recent years the main British colony, on the Ouse Washes of East Anglia, has suffered from

BAR-TAILED GODWIT
Limosa lapponica 38cm

This wader has a long, very slightly upturned, pink bill. Its winter plumage is a mottled grey-brown with a white rump showing as a V-shape in flight, and a barred tailed. The bar-tail is stockier and shorter legged than the slightly larger black-tail. It has a chestnut head and body in summer, although the underside of the wings remains white. Although the sexes are similar, it is possible to sort them out because the paler female has a longer bill than the male.

Breeding in the marshy tundra of Lapland and Russia, the bar-tailed godwit is usually seen in winter plumage in Britain where it is a winter visitor or a passage migrant to estuaries and mud flats, usually in loose flocks and not often with the other species. Looking hump backed when feeding, the bar-tailed godwit searches for food by probing the mud for worms, molluscs and crustaceans.

COMMON SANDPIPER

Actitis hypoleucos 20cm

Rather short legged and long bodied, the common sandpiper is a wader which breeds on upland rivers and beside Scottish lochs. Its head, which has a pale eye stripe, wings and tail are all olive-brown and its underparts are white apart from grey-brown breast patches.

Common sandpiper

Very active, the common sandpiper bobs its head and tail constantly as it searches for insects and other invertebrates. If disturbed, it flies on bowed wings with stiff wing-beats and a shrill 'twee-wee-wee'. It is a summer visitor to Wales, Scotland, northern England and Ireland, but it may be seen elsewhere on spring or autumn passage; very few remain in Britain all winter.

In late April and May, breeding common sandpipers perform display flights and sing loud, wickering songs. Their eggs are unusually large for the bird's size and well camouflaged in a grass-lined nest.

GREEN SANDPIPER

Tringa ochropus 23cm

The green sandpiper's dark plumage and white rump make it look rather like a large house martin in flight. Although it looks very similar to the wood sandpiper, it has darker, green-brown upperparts and shorter, dark legs. In flight the undersides of the wings are dark, unlike those of other similar waders.

This nervous, noisy bird has a twisting, erratic flight with a rapid climb after take off. Its 'keer-weet-weet' call is louder than the wood sandpiper's. Green sandpipers breed in Scandinavia and northern Russia and some winter in inland waters in the British Isles. If you see green sandpipers from April to June and from July to October they will be on passage between southern Europe and Africa and northern Europe.

WOOD SANDPIPER

Tringa glareola 20cm

The wood sandpiper is very like a green sandpiper but longer legged and more slender in form. It bobs its head and tail less than the shorter-legged common sandpiper. The bird is shy and flighty, often going away with a series of fast, high, peevish, 'chiff-iff-iff' calls. In flight it shows a similar pattern to a green sandpiper, but is much less contrasted, with a smaller white rump, browner wings and buffy-brown (instead of the green sandpiper's almost black) underwings.

It is a very rare breeding bird in Britain (a handful nest in Scotland) and only a scarce passage migrant in May and, more regularly, August and September. Most nest in Scandinavia and northern Russia and spend the winter in Africa.

Wood sandpiper

REDSHANK *Tringa totanus 28cm*

On the ground the redshank looks a middle-sized wader with a moderately long bill and legs and rather dark colours. Good views show that its legs are a vivid orange-red. Once it takes flight, however, it displays a striking white back and very broad white patches at the rear of its wings. In all probability it will also identify itself in flight by giving a series of loud, ringing 'teu-hu-hu' calls which unsettle every bird on the marsh.

Redshanks breed on saltmarshes and wet meadows, with a few on higher, damp heathland. Their courtship flights are noisy affairs and if eggs or young are threatened all the redshanks in an area join to mob the intruder with hysterical shouting cries. In winter the birds move to muddy estuaries where they feed in large but loose aggregations.

GREENSHANK *Tringa nebularia 32cm*

Taller and more graceful than the redshank, the greenshank has a long, slightly upturned bill and green legs. The head and underparts are pale, contrasting with its dark-grey back. In flight, which is swift and direct, the white back and rump show as a triangle, the body looks long and there is no white on the dark wings. It is easily alarmed and flies off with a ringing 'tow-tow-tow' call.

The greenshank is a summer visitor, breeding in small numbers on moorland in northern Scotland. Migrants from northern Europe are seen on inland waters in spring and autumn and a few remain on southern and western coasts throughout the winter. Its food is mainly invertebrates and small fish, caught by dashing about in shallow water to disturb them and then snatching them up in the bill.

RUFF *Philomachus pugnax 28cm*

In spring the male ruff is one of the most dramatic-looking birds in Britain, though sadly rare. Its colourful, loose ruff and ear tufts may be black, white, orange, grey, barred or plain. Groups of males gather at a 'lek' to fight and impress the dull, spotted females. In autumn and winter, males look duller, without any special fineries, often almost white on the head.

Ruff (male)

The females are browner and young birds in autumn (most commonly seen in Britain) are warm buff with beautiful buff and brown scaly patterns on their backs. They all have rather short, slightly curved bills, small heads on longish necks and long, yellowish or orange legs.

Ruffs are normally seen beside muddy lakes and reservoirs and on damp meadows. In flight they show only a thin white wing bar and white patches each side of the tail. Breeding is rare and irregular in Britain.

PURPLE SANDPIPER

Calidris maritima 21cm

Because it feeds among wet rocks and boulders the purple sandpiper, with its sooty, purplish-brown plumage, can be difficult to see, but it is tame and not uncommon around the rocky coasts of Britain and Ireland in winter. The upperparts are dark, the belly paler, the bill has an orange base and the legs are also orange.

Purple sandpiper

Narrow wing bars are noticeable in flight and there are white marks on either side of the black rump. Purple sandpipers fly low over the water and have a swift, dunlin-like action. Although often rather silent, they make a low 'weet-wit' call. They breed in Canada, Iceland, Greenland and Scandinavia and winter around the coasts of western Europe. They can be seen between September and April on British coasts, on rocks, reefs, breakwaters and boulders.

DUNLIN *Calidris alpina 18cm*

On any piece of shoreline from autumn to early spring the commonest wader is likely to be the dunlin. In good spots they may gather in hundreds, even thousands, spreading out over muddy and sandy shores at low tide and flocking together in dense packs as the tide rises and forces them to take refuge at an undisturbed roost. On a dull, cold winter's day they look rather dark and undistinguished, except for dull white undersides, though in flight as they twist and turn the flocks suddenly flash white beneath. Better views show a generally greyish-brown colour, short black legs and a slightly downcurved black bill. In flight they have a dark-centred tail and thin, but distinct, stripes of white along the wings.

Visit the same beach again in spring and a few may still be there, but by now they will be in lovely summer plumage, streaky grey on the head and breast, patterned with rusty-red, black and buff on top and, most distinctive of all, sporting a large rectangle of black on the belly. They may even sing from time to time, with a high, buzzy, trilling whistle.

Dunlin

In summer most dunlins move north to Scandinavia and beyond, but some remain to breed on the high ground of Wales, the Scottish moors and some coastal marshes in the Western Isles. During the autumn they are not uncommon on the shores of lakes and reservoirs inland. They have a rather nervous, hunched, shuffling action, not so tall and elegant as the larger ruff or redshank, nor so quick on the move as the sanderling.

SANDERLING *Calidris alba 20cm*

Lovely little sanderlings make life easy for the bird-watching beginner on a sandy shore, as they are easily approachable and almost unmistakable as they skitter about on twinkling feet, like clockwork toys. They rush after a receding wave to pick up tiny morsels swept aside by the sea, then scamper back up the beach again before the next breaker can sweep them off their feet. In winter they are silvery-grey on top and pure white below, with a short, straight, black bill and black legs. In spring a few may be seen in rich, mottled, rusty-brown plumage, remaining white beneath.

Sanderlings in flight have a pattern typical of many small waders, with a white-sided dark tail and dark wings with a long white central stripe, but the latter is much more eye-catching than on a dunlin. They call a short, sharp 'twick'. They nest right up in the Arctic Circle, staying in Britain until late May and returning again around late July or August.

Knot

KNOT *Calidris canutus 24cm*

Knots are 'middle-sized' waders, larger than a dunlin or ringed plover but smaller and shorter legged than a redshank. They are dull, pale grey, paler still below, but they tend to look darker at a distance. The best characteristic is often their remarkably social behaviour. Even on the most spacious beaches they will cram together in tight packs and feed in close ranks. When they roost at high tide they literally mass together shoulder to shoulder and several tens of thousands flock together in the few best estuaries like The Wash and Morecambe Bay. Elsewhere they are not especially common and inland they are always scarce.

In flight they are rather uniform, with a pale-grey rather than white rump. But the flight of a big flock of knots can be an awesome experience as the thousands of whirring wings give the impression of a swirling cloud of smoke. Lucky observers may find a few in spring which have already assumed summer plumage before flying off to the Arctic to nest. Then the dull, dumpy knot becomes a glorious bird of rich, orange-red.

A HUTCHINSON

GREAT SKUA *Stercorarius skua 56cm*

This large, dark-brown seabird, often known by its Shetland name of Bonxie, feeds by pirating fish caught by other birds. Although it looks slow and ponderous, the great skua can be very

Great skua

agile when it is chasing a gannet and trying to force it to regurgitate a recently caught fish. Not all its food is pirated: some fish are caught directly and other birds such as puffins and young gulls are also eaten. Skuas will also eat carrion found on beaches. Great skuas have broader wings than gulls and have white patches on the forewings which contrast vividly with the dark brown of the wings and body.

They breed in Iceland, the Faeroes, Orkney, Shetland, the Western Isles and the north of Scotland. In autumn they head south to subtropical seas and it is then that they may be seen elsewhere around the coasts.

When nesting they are very aggressive, flying at the heads of intruders into their territories, so it can be literally a hair-raising experience to venture into a breeding colony! Great skuas nest in colonies of between 30 and 100 pairs, laying two eggs on the ground. These are incubated mainly by the female, but it is the male which brings in almost all the food once the young have hatched.

GREAT BLACK-BACKED GULL

Larus marinus 71cm

Great black-backed gulls are almost as large as gannets and the most spectacular of our gulls. The head and bill are much heavier and the facial expression much fiercer than that of the lesser black-backed gull and the legs are pink, not yellow like those of the lesser black-back. In winter the head becomes only faintly streaked. Maturity is not reached for 4 or 5 years but the plumage changes of immatures are fairly easy to sort out. Juveniles are flecked brown and are both paler and larger than either the lesser black-backed and herring gulls, and after a year they begin to get black feathers above, a feature which instantly distinguishes them.

In winter great black-backs can be seen around the coast and on inland rubbish tips or roosting on reservoirs. Opportunistic feeders, they will eat carrion, other birds, refuse and fish. Breeding takes place at coastal sites varying from sea level to high cliffs, the nest usually in an imposing position. The nest is a mound of seaweed in which 2 or 3 eggs are laid. Both parents share the four-week incubation and care for the young through their seven-week fledging.

LESSER BLACK-BACKED GULL

Larus fuscus 60cm

This is one of the most elegant and handsome of our gulls, in summer, when it is immaculate white except for its slaty-grey back and wings. In winter the head and breast are heavily streaked. Its legs are yellow (duller in winter), unlike the great black-back or herring, but it has the same yellow bill with a red spot. Although longer winged and more finely built, it is a more voracious predator than the herring gull in summer, but equally willing to seek food on refuse tips in the winter.

Young birds are dark, mottled brown; the young herring gull has a paler patch behind the bend of the wing in flight which this species lacks. Lesser black-backed colonies are often in beautiful places like the flowery islands of south-west Wales, where the gulls look superb in a setting of bluebells, red and sea campion and thrift. They leave these places in the autumn and used to migrate to Africa. Many still do, but increasing numbers have chosen to remain here in winter, living inland, foraging at tips and roosting on reservoirs every night.

HERRING GULL *Larus argentatus 61cm*

The most familiar 'seaside' gull is the noisy one which calls from the guest house roof at dawn all summer through, snatches sandwiches from people on the pier and generally makes a nuisance of itself around the fish quays. But in winter, when it lives in flocks on the coast and also far inland, it becomes more aloof, wary and often hard to approach.

It is a large, grey and white gull, with a pale blue-grey or silvery back and sharp black and white wingtips. Its legs are pale pink and the bill is yellow with a red spot, the 'target' for chicks to peck at to stimulate parent gulls into regurgitating food for them.

Herring gulls nest on slopes and cliffs beside the sea, and increasingly on roofs of buildings in places like Bristol, but forage almost anywhere, from the top of Snowdon where scraps left by tourists give them a living, to any piece of shoreline, and on rubbish tips in winter. They like fish, shellfish and crabs and just about anything else that might be edible.

Herring gull

COMMON GULL *Larus canus 41cm*

This is like a smaller, more delicate version of the herring gull, with a very similar pattern but slightly darker back. It has a slimmer bill of yellow-green, without a red spot, and green legs. Young birds are neatly patterned in brown, grey and white. They are best identified in flight, when their tails look pure white except for a sharp, broad band of black at the tip. Common gull calls are much more whining or squealing than the familiar sounds of the herring gull.

Common gull

In summer common gulls are not actually very common except in Scotland, but they are far more widespread (though still patchy) in winter. Then they join other gulls at tips, though they are really most at home on pastures and playing fields where they can search for insects and worms in the short turf.

BLACK-HEADED GULL
Larus ridibundus 36cm

Despite its name, the 'hood' of the adult in summer is a dark, chocolate-brown, and in winter and immature plumages the head is white except for a dark spot behind the eye. Much better as an identification feature is the pattern on the wing. The outer half has a line of black along the trailing edge, and a broad triangle of white along the front, which flashes an eye-catching and easy clue to identity even at very long range. Black-headed gulls are unlike other common species of gull in having red legs and bill (dark in summer, more scarlet in winter) and they are also the smallest and most agile of the numerous gulls. Young birds have paler, more orange legs at first, and browner marks on wings and tail.

They breed beside shallow lakes and marshes, and also high on western moors, making a thick pad of rushes and grass on which to lay their mottled brown eggs. A colony is a noisy, lively place full of energy and aggression, and gulls gang together to swoop at the head of an intruder. These gulls are abundant and widespread, difficult to miss even when in the car or on a train journey.

Black-headed gull

LITTLE GULL *Larus minutus 26cm*

The little gull is smaller than other gulls. The smoky-grey underwings are fringed with a white edge and may look very dark in some lights. In winter the black on the head (a summer marking) disappears to be

Little gull

replaced by white with a grey smudge on the nape. Immature birds have dark W-shaped marks across the wings. Little gulls are mainly spring and autumn migrants to British coasts and are seen on reservoirs inland, lakes near the coast and a few parts of the Irish and North Sea shores.

KITTIWAKE *Larus tridactyla 39cm*

Kittiwakes breed in large colonies, their tiny nests clinging to ledges on sheer cliffs. With guillemots and other species as near neighbours, they constitute great seabird cities. The kittiwake in such a place, where it noisily calls its name, 'kitt-i-a-ake', is unmistakable, and is seen at its best from April to August. In winter, isolated birds need to be distinguished from the similar-sized common gull. They are grey on top, white beneath, but have triangular wing tip patches of solid black, as if dipped in ink, without white spots. Young birds are easy to spot, having no brown, but a zigzag band of black across the wings.

Kittiwakes are much more truly seabirds than most gulls, living far out over the oceans except when nesting, and they are never seen in fields or at refuse tips. They nest mainly in north-east England, Scotland's east and north coasts and the northern isles.

GUILLEMOT *Uria aalge 41cm*

The guillemot looks the nearest bird we have to a penguin. It is much smaller than most penguins, however, and able to fly fast and direct, though its narrow, small wings beat furiously and it is never capable of much aerial agility. The guillemot is brown on the head and back (northern birds are darker), with white underparts. The bill is slim and pointed, ideal for catching fish underwater.

Guillemots breed on large cliffs, using small horizontal ledges and making no nest. They are found mainly in the north-east, north and a few western localities, and the biggest colonies run into many thousands of birds. As soon as the chick is half grown it leaps from the cliff, with its father in attendance, then swims off out to sea, usually in July. The birds remain out at sea all winter.

Guillemot

RAZORBILL *Alca torda 40cm*

Stockier and blacker above than the
guillemot, the razorbill has a more pointed
tail, often evident when swimming. More
obvious at close range is the deeper, blade-
like bill, which is crossed by a white line in
front of the eye. Razorbills are often found

Razorbill

on the same cliffs as guillemots, but
usually in smaller numbers and generally
they are less obvious. They prefer to nest
in cavities and at the back of deeper
ledges, living a quieter, less argumentative
life. Like guillemots, they lay a single egg
on bare rock. It takes five weeks to hatch
but the chick leaves the ledge after only
about 18 days, fluttering to the sea when
only half grown. It is a dangerous time for
the young razorbill, with gulls and skuas
eager to snatch up baby birds.

Razorbills return to land in late
spring, and leave again by late summer.
The rest of the time they are at sea, though
often closer to land than guillemots and
sometimes in sheltered bays and estuaries.
They dive from the surface of the sea to
catch fish.

PUFFIN *Fratercula arctica 28cm*

With its enormous, bright, multicoloured
bill and neat, round, black and white body,
the puffin is one of the best-known
seabirds, although to be sure of seeing
one, you need to visit a breeding colony in
spring or summer. The body is so plump
and the wings so narrow that it can be
hard to believe that the puffin can fly, and
it is easy to understand why the wing-
beats are so very rapid. In winter the bill
becomes smaller and dull and the face
changes from white to grey.

The puffin catches the small fish on
which it feeds by diving from the surface
and swimming underwater using its
wings. Puffins spend more time at sea
than on land, coming ashore only to breed.
They nest in burrows in grassy sea cliffs
on western and northern coasts, arriving
in early spring and leaving in late summer.
Only one egg is laid and although both
parents care for the chick, they leave it
after about six weeks and it then has to
make its own way out of its burrow and
plunge off the cliff top into the sea.

Lesser black-backed gull

Great black-backed gull

Kittiwake

Puffin

Common tern

Turtle dove

Collared dove

Woodpigeon

Barn owl

Tawny owl

Green woodpecker (female)

Nightjar (female)

Kingfisher

Swallow

Chough

Jay

Great tit

Marsh tit

Redwing

Dipper

Fieldfare

COMMON TERN *Sterna hirundo 33cm*

A tern colony is a noisy, lively place, where the birds are all highly strung, excitable and aggressive. Common terns are indeed the commonest terns in most of Britain (though far less numerous than Arctic terns in the far north) and the most likely species to be seen inland, where some breed beside flooded gravel pits and feed along larger rivers.

Common tern

Like a small, slender, long-tailed gull with pointed wings, the common tern is pale grey and white, with a jet-black cap. Its bill is orange-red with a black tip, its short legs bright red. The outer parts of its wings are darker streaked (unlike the Arctic's and often the best means of telling them apart). The underwing shows a broad, dusky trailing edge towards the tip (much narrower in the Arctic tern) and a pale, translucent triangle behind the bend of the wing. On the Arctic tern all the long wing feathers are light and translucent and it looks a paler, daintier, slimmer-winged bird in flight. Both species catch fish by hovering over water, then diving in head-first from a height, with a loud splash.

Common terns are widespread in Europe in summer and migrate far south for the winter, into southern tropical seas. They leave here in October and return in April. They nest on the ground, mostly in colonies on the coast, on sandy or shingly beaches, islands in shallow lagoons or on offshore rocks.

ARCTIC TERN *Sterna paradisaea 33cm*

Arctic terns look very like common terns, but adults in summer have shorter, darker red bills, shorter legs (easy to see when they stand together, as they frequently do), longer tails and more slender wings which are cleaner grey on top and purer white below. In late summer, common terns have white foreheads; Arctics usually keep a full black cap until after they leave Britain in the autumn.

They are commonest in northern Britain and breed far north into the Arctic. In autumn they embark on a 20,000-mile trip that will take them to the fringes of the Antarctic before they return in April. Like common terns they nest on rocky islands and sandy beaches, but not inland. Terns at a colony are noisy, with rasping 'ki-airr' and 'kiki-kik' calls, and are aggressive to any intruder — such as a fox. They will strike human visitors on the head, drawing blood with their sharp beaks, and are easily disturbed, so, all in all, it is best to keep well away from their nests.

Arctic tern

A HUTCHINSON

LITTLE TERN *Sterna albifrons 23cm*

The little tern really is small compared with other sea terns and tiny beside any of the gulls. It has a long pointed yellow bill with a black tip and there is a noticeable white forehead with a narrow black line from the eye to the bill in early spring. The orange-yellow legs are short and the profile of a standing bird is squat. In flight, however, it is very delicate with long, dark-tipped wings, a short forked tail and rather dumpy body. Flight is hurried with very quick wing-beats and when fishing it hovers on rapidly moving wings with head held low before it plunges. The calls of the little tern include a sharp 'kit-kit' and a grating 'kee-rick'.

The birds feed close inshore on small fish, sand-eels and crustaceans, but they will also catch insects on the wing. They are summer visitors from April to October. Because they choose sandy and shingle beaches for their colonies, they are very vulnerable to accidental damage by unaware holidaymakers, a case of the excellent camouflage of the eggs and young leading to destruction rather than protection. British and Irish populations have diminished alarmingly over the last 20 years or so.

Little tern

SANDWICH TERN
Sterna sandvicensis 39cm

This is the largest and palest British tern, much whiter beneath than the common or Arctic, more shaggily crested on the back of its head and with a unique black bill with a small yellow tip. Its legs are also black. Sandwich terns return to Britain

Sandwich tern

from African coasts in March and April and stay until September. They nest mainly on the east coasts, on sand dunes and shingle spits, usually in nature reserves where they are free from disturbance from holidaymakers enjoying the seaside. Almost all are in a few large colonies and small, isolated groups are far less likely than with the common or Arctic. They lay two spotted eggs in May.

Fishing Sandwich terns dive in with a special vehemence, striking the water with a loud smack as they plunge on to a sand-eel or other small fish. Feeding groups are often very obvious offshore (especially off shelving shingle banks and in large, sandy bays), drawing attention to themselves by their loud, two- (almost three-) syllable calls, a rasping 'kierrink' or 'kirrick'.

CUCKOO *Cuculus canorus 33cm*

The male cuckoo is far more often heard than seen, and its well-known call must be the most welcome sound of spring for many people. The female's call, less familiar than the male's, sounds like bubbling water. The cuckoo has a grey back, head and upper breast with a finely barred breast and belly. Sexes are alike, except that females have brown-tinged underparts, and immatures are rufous brown. In flight the cuckoo looks like a bird of prey, but it has a thinner head, noticeably rounded and spotted tail and long, pointed, swept-back wings. The bird, a summer visitor to the British Isles, is found in a variety of habitats — woodland, parkland, scrub, farmland, heathland, reed beds and moorland.

Cuckoos are best known as nest parasites, laying eggs in the nests of other, smaller birds. Each female tends to specialise in a particular host species and her eggs match those of the chosen host. About 100 different hosts have been recorded, but the most frequent in Britain are meadow pipits, reed warblers and dunnocks. To make way for her own egg, the female will remove one of the host's. The cuckoo's egg hatches quickly in about 11 days and the young cuckoo pushes the remaining eggs or other chicks out of the

Cuckoo removing egg from nest

TURTLE DOVE
Streptopelia turtur 27cm

This is a lovely little dove, neat, delicate and beautifully patterned, though a close view is needed to appreciate the subtle details. It has a grey head and pink breast, a patch of grey and white streaks on the side of the neck, and pale chestnut-brown back and wings, each feather with a blackish central patch. In flight it shows a blue-grey patch on each wing and the tail is long, rather pointed, with a broad white band across the tip.

Its soothing, purring calls are an essential part of the rural scene in a fine English summer — rolling 'puurrrr puurrrr' notes, given from the depths of a large bush or hedge. Turtle doves love bushy old elders and hawthorns. They are in Britain only from April to September (so, at other times, small doves are likely to be collared doves).

nest. Fledging takes 19 days, but the young cuckoo is fed by its foster parents (which it often dwarfs) for three weeks or more and it makes the trip to Africa several weeks after its real parents have migrated.

WOODPIGEON
Columba palumbus 41cm

Woodpigeons have almost every man's hand against them but still manage to be common, even abundant, one of the few species legitimately labelled 'pest'. Yet, despite being shot in thousands in woods and over fields, woodpigeons are ready to become tame and familiar when unmolested, as in a city park. It is then that the real beauty of the bird is best appreciated, for the woodpigeon, a big, bulky bird, is subtly patterned in pale greys, pink and brown, with distinctive splashes of white on each side of the neck and broad white bands crossing the wings in flight. Young birds have these wing patches, but not the neck spots at first.

A disturbed woodpigeon clatters off at great speed, using all the power of its broad wings and deep breast muscles — which is why it is 'pigeon-chested' — to make a fast escape. Few birds are stronger fliers. The nest is a flat, skimpy effort in a tree or bush.

Woodpigeon

FERAL PIGEON/ROCK DOVE
Columbia livia 33cm

Wild rock doves are very widely spread throughout Europe and North Africa and are the source of the domesticated pigeon which now appears in such forms as homing and racing pigeons, fantails and the wild-living domestic pigeons of our towns and waste places. Many of these 'feral' birds have returned to live with true

Feral pigeon

rock doves and have interbred, so the 'pure' strain of rock dove has disappeared from most places. Only in the far north of Scotland and on the outer isles can 'true' rock doves be seen, neat blue-grey birds with paler backs, big white rump patches, white underwings and two bars of black across the top of each wing. They are beautiful and dramatic birds as they swoop into a sea cave at the foot of a great cliff, above crashing waves, and too easily dismissed as 'just pigeons'. Feral birds can look nearly identical, or patched with black or white, or rusty-red, usually also much more scruffy.

Rock doves live on sea cliffs. The ledges of town buildings and quarries do just as well for feral pigeons. They eat green food and seeds in 'wilder' areas, more scraps and bread in towns, where they add a touch of life and colour but are intensely disliked by most local authorities because of the mess and perceived health hazards they cause.

COLLARED DOVE

Streptopelia decaocto 32cm

The rather dull-looking collared dove is at the centre of one of the most dramatic, and still unexplained, spreads of range of any bird. It was restricted to Middle Eastern countries until the 1930s but moved rapidly westwards until it first bred in the British Isles in 1955. Today it is very common and widespread. It can be seen in farmland, gardens, parks and around waste ground such as railway yards — anywhere where it can find spilled grain, and where there are occasional bushy conifers in which it can hide its flimsy nest. But it avoids open cereal fields, dense woodland and cities.

STOCK DOVE *Columba oenas 35cm*

Whereas woodpigeons are abundant and easily seen and collared doves are often in gardens, stock doves remain rather aloof and unknown to most people. They are not uncommon but are simply overlooked as 'pigeons', being about the same size and shape as a homing pigeon. A stock dove is smaller and rounder than a woodpigeon, and more blue-grey, less brown, with no white patches.

Stock dove

It is larger, longer tailed and heavier than a turtle dove, much less colourful and basically a pale, greyish-fawn or dull pinkish-brown. The wing tips are dark and blue-grey areas show well in flight, but the best features are the tail, which is black with a broad white tip when seen from underneath, and the thin half-ring of black over the back of the neck. In fact it is easily detected even if not seen, by its monotonous triple song — 'cu-coo-cuk'.

In flight it is swift and direct, showing paler-grey wings with blacker edgings and grey under the wing (often white in a feral pigeon). It is subtly different in shape from other pigeons, with a shorter tail and a rounder head. Stock doves nest in cavities in old trees, so prefer old, open woodland and parks and farmland with big trees in the hedges. Cavities are also found in some sea cliffs and inland crags, and these are occupied by doves provided that suitable feeding places are nearby. Stock doves eat grain, seeds, buds and sweet, green leaves, and feed in fields or woodland clearings.

BARN OWL *Tyto alba 34cm*

The barn owl is a general favourite which no one persecutes, yet it is in decline and has been for 50 years. Climatic change, and especially a series of cold, snowy winters, can cause a drop in numbers, but it seems to be agricultural intensification that is really behind the change in fortunes of this lovely bird. It needs old outhouses and barns with access through a hole or open window, or big, hollow trees in which to nest, and these 'untidy' features are ever harder to find. But more than that, it needs food — small voles, rats and mice, which live in the rough grassland and bushy places now so rare on much of our farmland. Cereal prairies are disastrous for barn owls, as the disturbed fields, which suffer regular ploughing, spraying, harvesting and burning, have nothing to offer in the way of prey. Many owls turn to roadside verges, with catastrophic results as the number of traffic victims will show.

Barn owls look white in the headlights of a car at night, but are really only white underneath and beautifully patterned with grey peppering on a golden-buff upperside. They have rather monkey-like, heart-shaped faces and long legs with 'knock-knees'. When hunting, they catch voles or mice in a short, headlong dive, sometimes after a brief hover. A hunting owl is always fascinating to watch and barn owls do come out before dark, often in the same place for several evenings in succession, when they are feeding young in midsummer. They may be abroad in daylight on freezing winter's days, too, when life is difficult for them.

LONG-EARED OWL *Asio otus 36cm*

This splendidly patterned owl, with fiery orange eyes and long tufts of feathers on its head (not 'ears' at all), is little known, being very secretive, extremely nocturnal and quiet. Its 'song' is a soft, almost cooing, moaning hoot.

Long-eared owls are scattered thinly over most of Britain (and are the common owls in Ireland). They nest in coniferous forests, near the edge because they feed over open ground, and in thickets of hawthorn. They make no nest of their own but take over the old nest of a crow, or a squirrel's drey. In winter they are more numerous, with immigrants from the Continent, and roost in thick hedges and thickets of willows and thorns, as well as in woodland sites.

Long-eared owl

TAWNY OWL *Strix aluco 30cm*

By far the commonest owl, the big, broad tawny is the one which will sit on a chimney top or in a dark tree on the edge of a town park at night, making the long, tremulous and beautiful 'hoot'. The description scarcely does justice to the sound. The common call of the tawny owl is a sharp, urgent 'ke-wick' and young

Tawny owl

birds on a late summer evening can set up a remarkable chorus of unearthly shouts and wails based on this call. It is the 'ke-wick' which gives the popular 'tu-wit' to the 'tu-woo' but, contrary to traditional belief, the call and the hoot are not really heard in combination in that way.

Tawnies are big birds but easily missed as they spend the day in a tree, often an evergreen oak, a pine or in thick ivy, where they are very hard to spot. If they are found by small birds a whole flock of angry tits, finches and thrushes may gather, shouting at the owl, and this may give it away. They hunt only at night, flying to a more open perch to watch for voles, rats, small birds and all sorts of smaller fry. Tawny owls nest in holes in trees, in buildings and even in holes in the ground.

SHORT-EARED OWL

Asio flammeus 38cm

This large, long-winged owl breeds on northern moors and in plantations of young conifers, on a few western coasts and islands and more sparsely on the dunes and marshes of the east coast of England. In winter it is more common, and visits many areas of heath and rough pasture. It can be seen hunting in the daytime more than other owls and flies low over the ground with soft, shallow wing-beats and short glides. Then it looks pale, mostly buffy-brown, with characteristic dark patches on the wings and creamy areas near the wing tips. Its eyes gleam yellow, surrounded by black, giving a fierce, alert expression.

Short-eared owls nest on the ground in heather, rushes or tall grass. They eat voles and the number of eggs they lay, and young that survive, depend on the abundance of their food.

Short-eared owl

LITTLE OWL *Athene noctua 22cm*

Little owls, introduced into Britain in the late 19th century, are now common as far north as the Borders. The introduction was, perhaps rightly, deemed unwelcome, but the reasons for the outcry were false. It was claimed that little owls ate gamebird chicks. Studies showed that they actually ate worms, beetles, moths and mice.

The little owl hunts at night but is often seen by day, simply sitting on an obvious perch such as a dead branch or a fence post. It looks thickset and broad headed, bigger than its length suggests, and in flight its broad wings increase the apparent size. But it is by far the smallest owl and its yellow eyes, beetling brows and streaked and spotted grey-brown plumage make it easy to identify. It inhabits parkland and farmland where there are still plentiful trees, and nests in a hole in a tree or broken, rotten branch.

Little owl

KINGFISHER *Alcedo atthis 16cm*

To someone seeing it for the first time, the kingfisher usually looks surprisingly small, but there is no denying its glorious colour. Nevertheless, as it sits still in an overhanging spray of leaves above a sparkling stream, the play of light and shade and reflections make it very difficult to see despite its orange, blue, green and

Kingfisher

white pattern. When it flies it is often more conspicuous, first of all giving a clue to its presence with a high-pitched, shrill whistle and showing a streak of electric blue along its back as it darts away, low over the water.

Kingfishers catch fish after spying them from a perch, or, if there are no suitable perches on a modern 'canalised' river, by hovering. The water must, therefore, be clear and not too fast flowing. For its nest the kingfisher needs a small cliff of earth over water, a sheer bank which will prevent predators from reaching it. The bird digs a long, horizontal tunnel 90—180cm into the bank and lays 6 or 7 eggs on a bed of fish bones. Kingfishers are widespread, but never very common, in both England and Wales, and rare throughout Scotland.

GREAT SPOTTED WOODPECKER

Dendrocopos major 23cm

Our commonest and most widespread woodpecker, of both broadleaved and coniferous woods, the lively great spotted woodpecker is a thrush-sized, stockily built bird. It is frequently located by first hearing its sharp, loud 'tchick' call, then by seeing it fly from the middle of a tree and crossing a clearing in a series of switchback dips and bounds.

Such a view is often enough to show its bold black and white pattern, with a large white patch at the base of each wing; a glimpse of vivid red beneath the tail will confirm its identification. Lucky people may see one at a garden bird feeder, raiding the peanut bag or taking bits of suspended fat or cheese; then it can be seen to be a most splendid bird.

Typical of woodpeckers, it feeds on insects and their larvae from beneath loose bark or even by tunnelling into solid wood, as it can chip into a large branch with ease. In early spring it makes a very loud, abrupt 'drum', rattling its bill so quickly against a resonant branch that the sound is almost like a loud bark. In May it digs a small hole into a vertical trunk and lays up to seven round, white eggs inside on a bed of chippings.

Great spotted woodpecker

LESSER SPOTTED WOODPECKER

Dendrocopos minor 15cm·

This tiny woodpecker is more at home fluttering about from twig to twig at the very top of a deciduous tree than hammering the bark of a big, solid tree trunk in classic woodpecker fashion.

Lesser spotted woodpecker (male)

Because of its far less bold and obvious life style, it is seen much less than other woodpeckers, and in most areas is actually scarcer. It is rare in northern England and does not live in Scotland. The best chance of spotting one is in early spring, when the high, rapid, peevish calls — sounding like 'pee-pee-pee-peepee' — may be heard occasionally. Even then, it needs a sharp eye to spot the bird before it flies away, to call again from a far distant tree several minutes later.

It is a black and white bird but without the bold, clear-white patches of the bigger great spotted woodpecker, nor the bright red beneath the tail. Instead it has a rather blurred pattern of horizontal bars across its back; the male has a red cap. It makes a weaker, but slightly longer, drumming sound than its relative. Its nest hole, much smaller in diameter, is usually bored into a smaller, higher branch.

GREEN WOODPECKER
Picus viridis 32cm

From parts of Fife and central Scotland southwards, the green woodpecker's loud, ringing, almost laughing voice is a characteristic sound of old woodland with clearings and bushy heaths. To many, however, the call is a disembodied voice, and the bird itself is not at all familiar.

It feeds mostly on the ground, looking for ants, although it has the typical woodpecker shape and strong tail which it uses as a prop to support it against an upright branch or the trunk of a tree, and a sharp, chisel bill with which it excavates its nest hole. The bird takes people by surprise when scared up from the ground, when it flies off with a deeply swooping, undulating action and shows its vivid-yellow lower back. Should it settle in a tree it will often cleverly perch around the back of a branch out of sight, or sit very still and be difficult to spot, but a good view will reveal an apple-green bird, paler beneath, with a black patch around its pale eye and a broad cap of crimson.

SKYLARK *Alauda arvensis 18cm*

Although a small bird, between a sparrow and a starling in size, the skylark is broadly built and has a noticeably 'in between' look about it, not so small as most of the sparrows and finches of the fields. In flight the broad, angular wings enhance the impression of size. If seen flying away, its white-edged tail looks relatively short and the wings have a noticeable white trailing edge. Otherwise, it is brown and streaky, and has a tiny, blunt crest.

The chief feature of the skylark is its glorious song. It inhabits wide, open spaces, from upland moors and high plateaux to low agricultural land, all places with no suitable high perch for a songbird. Instead, it rises vertically upwards, hovering as a tiny dot high in the sky, singing its heart out in a continuous outpouring of rapid, beautiful warbling, which seems thinner and higher pitched with greater distance.

The skylark is one of the most widely distributed of all Britain's birds, found practically everywhere except in enclosed urban land and woods. There may be several million pairs of them altogether, widely scattered except in winter when they join together and roam in flocks up to a few hundred strong.

Skylark

NIGHTJAR *Caprimulgus europaeus 27cm*
Southern heathlands with scattered trees
are the nightjar's preferred home. It arrives
from Africa in May and leaves by late
August. It feeds at twilight on moths, and
the male has a remarkable song, a
prolonged, rapid, hollow churring a little
like the sound of a distant, low-pitched,
two-stroke motorcycle. Nightjars are long
winged and long tailed, with wide mouths
but tiny bills.

Swift

The birds may be found in big flocks
over lakes and reservoirs whenever there is
a storm, avoiding the worst of the weather
and searching for concentrations of tiny
flies. The swift is all blackish-brown, with
very long, narrow scythe-like wings. It is
the bird which flies around houses in
summer, making piercing, screeching calls.

SWALLOW *Hirundo rustica 18cm*
Much of the length of this bird is made up
by its long outer tail feathers. Its graceful
form, deeply forked tail and low, rather
direct, swooping flight make it a universal
favourite. Unlike the swift, it has rather
broad-based wings, and shows a lot of
colour if seen well — steely blue on top,
cream or pinkish beneath, with patches of
deep red on the face.

Nightjar

SWIFT *Apus apus 16cm*
This is an astonishing bird, for a young
swift will leave its nest inside the roof of
an old house in August, then fly south to
Africa and not return to Britain for three
years. During that time it probably never
comes to a perch, but spends its whole life
on the wing. Even in Britain, where the
swift arrives in May and is gone before
September, it comes down only to its nest.
It feeds by catching aerial insects in its
wide mouth. It collects most material on
the wing and also sleeps on the wing, if it
sleeps at all, and may even mate in midair.

It perches on aerials and wires, and
will select a suitable perch to sing from —
the song is a pleasant twittering with a
distinctive low trill in the middle. The
swift has its nest hidden deep in a cavity,
but the swallow prefers a beam in a shed
or barn, just under the roof.

Swallows spend the winter near the
very tip of South Africa but return to
Britain each April after an arduous
migration; they leave again in September.
They feed entirely on insects caught in
flight, so rarely, if ever, survive a winter
in this country.

HOUSE MARTIN *Delichon urbica 13cm*

This little bird is easily distinguished from swallows and swifts by its pure-white underside and the bold, square patch of white just above its tail. The round nests of dried mud are equally distinctive, and the presence of a colony on a house, tucked up beneath the eaves, is usually welcome, if not the inevitable mess on the ground below.

House martin

House martins are mysterious birds, for no one really knows their whereabouts in winter. They go to tropical Africa but probably spend most of their time high in the air, almost out of sight. In Britain they are easy to see, though they do feed higher up than swallows, often over new housing estates. They make dry, twittering noises, less musical than the swallow's.

Sometimes house martins raise several broods in a summer and may still have young birds in the nest when they should be heading south at the end of September — occasionally they will leave and desert the chicks in the nest. Gatherings of martins on wires and rooftops, where they will often bask in warm sunshine, are usually of this species.

SAND MARTIN *Riparia riparia 12cm*

Unlike the swallow and house martin, this, the smallest martin, is a brown and white bird, without the glistening blues and eye-catching white patches of the others. It is also a bird of river banks, quarries and gravel workings, not of the suburbs or farm buildings, as it feeds on insects over water and nests by burrowing deep into a vertical bank of earth or sand.

The sand martin is an early spring arrival, often reaching England in mid-March, and is found all over Britain. Flocks gather to roost in reed beds in September, before heading back south. The bird used to be very much more common, but its numbers have been drastically reduced — perhaps by 80 or 90 per cent — because of the tragic drought in the Sahel. It is in this region, south of the Sahara, that the species spends the winter, and it is simply unable to survive there, or to fly back across the widening desert.

Sand martin

RAVEN *Corvus corax 63cm*

Our biggest, toughest crow, this splendid bird is very widespread in the northern hemisphere, living in all kinds of conditions from near desert to Arctic tundra and sea cliffs. In Britain it is rather artificially confined to the hills and coasts of the north and west, having been pushed back to the wilderness areas by

Raven

persecution in the past. Though now in no danger, enough anti-raven (or anti-crow) feeling persists to prevent its spread back into the hills of the Midlands and the Pennines and the wilder areas of the New Forest or East Anglia, where it would undoubtedly be at home.

It is a very big bird, but size is deceptive in its spacious environment, and shape is a better clue. Compared with a rook or crow it is longer winged, with a more protruding head (often exaggerated by its big bill and puffed-out throat feathers), and a longer, almost diamond-shaped tail. It tends to fly at a greater height and is capable of breathtaking aerobatics, often rolling over on to its back in midair.

It has loud, metallic and barking calls. The raven nests on cliffs and also in big trees, laying eggs early in the year while there may still be snow over its bleak home range.

CARRION CROW *Corvus corone 46cm*

Much bigger than a pigeon, this is a large, solidly built bird with a stout beak, though far less formidable than a raven. It is very much more widespread, often to be seen beside motorways and other roads foraging for dead rabbits and other traffic victims, even insects. Crows usually go about in ones and twos but can form flocks, though they are less likely to be seen in hundreds on agricultural land than are rooks.

The crow is black faced and has a neater, tighter plumage than the more ragged, bare-faced rook. It eats almost anything and is persecuted by farmers and gamekeepers more than any other bird — yet it is wily enough to survive almost undiminished. Its success is explained by its adaptability and, maybe, by its undoubted intelligence.

Carrion crow

Crows nest in tall trees, making a solitary nest of big sticks. Their eggs are greenish with dark blotches. They remain in their nesting area all year round though some will come down from the exposed moors for easier pickings in the valleys in the worst of the winter weather.

HOODED CROW
Corvus corone cornix 46cm

The hooded crow is an interesting example of a 'subspecies', or race, in this case a race of the more familiar southern carrion crow. It is simply the form of a crow that replaces the all-black type in Ireland, the Isle of Man and most of northern and western Scotland, though, where the two meet in central Scotland, there is a narrow belt of 'mixed' crows halfway between the two forms.

The hoodie is a smart bird, grey with black head, chest, tail and wings, and seems to have an even less enviable reputation than the carrion crow. Even so, objective studies of hoodies in Scotland

Hooded crow

have shown that they are more likely to steal food from the cattle byre than to kill a lamb. Many actually get their living by foraging on rubbish tips.

Like the carrion crow, the bird makes a big nest of sticks, sometimes on a crag. It has the same unforgiving, grating caw. Hooded crows from Scandinavia move south in winter and sometimes appear in eastern England, especially near the coast.

ROOK *Corvus frugilegus 45cm*

The rook, though it might take a little surplus grain, is a much more pleasant character, on the whole, than the carrion crow. With its bare grey face, baggy 'trousers' and tendency to live all its life in flocks, the sociable rook is fairly easy to tell from other crows. In flight it has rounder wings and a much more rounded tip to its tail than a crow, and its voice is a more pleasant, amiable cawing.

Rooks nest in colonies, from a handful of pairs to several hundred together, all over Britain where there is agricultural land. Flocks visit the moors but it is not a bird of the hills on the whole. The tree-top nests, sizeable affairs made up of thick sticks, are occupied in early spring with a great deal of loud cawing and frequent ringing, even bugling notes. There is a lot of stealing of sticks and general rowdiness in the colony, but rooks always seem to feed quietly together when they fly out to the fields.

Rook

Rooks have declined in places, probably due to farming activities which make it less easy for them to find a plentiful supply of earthworms — vast acreages of sprayed cereal fields are not in the best interests of this species, which requires more permanent pasture and stretches of ploughed stubble.

JACKDAW *Corvus monedula 33cm*

This lively little crow is about the size of a pigeon. It is at home in agricultural areas (where it often hangs about with rooks), in open woods where old trees provide holes in which it can nest, and in parks where it can feed on short turf and nest in the cavities of big, old buildings; it also inhabits quarries and cliffs, whether on hills or beside the sea. Yet there are inexplicable gaps in its distribution.

Jackdaw

On the ground, it looks a much lighter, perkier bird than a carrion crow or rook. It is best identified by the contrast of the black face and cap with a much greyer neck. Its white eye is a noticeable feature at close range. In flight, it has a quicker action than a carrion crow, again more reminiscent of a pigeon, with its wings looking rather rounded. The frequent sharp, almost squeaky 'chak' or 'jack' sounds from a flying bird also make it easy to identify.

Jackdaws feed on the ground, searching for worms, grubs and leatherjackets. They will eat almost anything they can catch, from mice to beetles, and frequently join rooks and crows at refuse tips.

CHOUGH *Pyrrhocorax pyrrhocorax 38cm*

Few birds give the impression of the chough's bounce, vivacity and energy. It is a rare, specialised crow which lives on the coastal cliffs of west Wales, Ireland, the Isle of Man and a very few Scottish islands. In winter, local populations gather together in joyful flocks that bound across the sky in fast, acrobatic flight.

It is the recent transformation of heathland above coastal cliffs into farmland that has led to the demise of the chough in many areas. It needs short turf and thin soil over outcropping rocks, in which it can probe for ants, and fertilised fields do not offer it a good substitute.

Chough

A few pairs live in man-made places — Welsh slate quarries and deep down in mine shafts — but these do little to balance the losses. Very often choughs are found with jackdaws. Compared with a jackdaw, or a rook, the chough is more slender, but much broader and squarer in the wing. Its long, curved bill and legs are bright red, unique for a crow. It is a noisy bird, with loud, powerful, high-pitched calls that echo around the cliffs — all too rarely heard by most of us nowadays.

JAY *Garrulus glandarius 34cm*

Few people would recognise this bird as being one of the crow family. Instead of sombre black and grey, it is clothed in soft pink, black, white and brilliant blue, though the blue patch on each wing is not easy to see. More often it is seen as a bird that flies off, deep into the heart of a wood, giving a hoarse, screeching call and showing a big patch of white on its rump.

MAGPIE *Pica pica 45cm*

The magpie is unmistakable, with its glossy black and striking white pattern, long, tapered tail and machine-gun-rattle voice. It declined through persecution in the past but has recently staged a marked revival. This has not met with universal approval — in fact, few birds are so controversial. The most sympathetic bird lover seems to want to eradicate the magpie if one should raid a nest in his or her garden. It is a sad sight to see small

Magpie

Jays live in thick woodland, including many coniferous plantations. Most of all they are associated with oaks, and, indeed, it is probable that oakwoods have spread in the past because of the attentions of the jay. Heavy acorns will not get far unless carried, and jays carry thousands and thousands of them from oaks to bury in soft soil elsewhere.

They are remarkably good at remembering where the acorns are and retrieve many in the winter, and even feed their young on them next spring. But inevitably some are left, and grow into oak saplings. Though they eat so many acorns, and otherwise take mainly caterpillars, jays do take a few eggs and young birds, though not nearly so many as sparrowhawks, or cats, and yet are savagely persecuted for it. They deserve better treatment, for few birds are so lovely to look at.

birds robbed of eggs and chicks, but the magpie has no overall effect on the numbers of songbirds in the long run.

The magpie makes a nest of thick sticks, deep in a hawthorn hedge or in the top of a tree. The nest has a big, densely woven cup topped by a looser dome of protective sticks, making it easy to see in the winter months as a large, round, black mass. Young magpies look like their parents, except that at first they have a rather shorter tail.

Stonechat (male)

Redstart (male)

Wheatear (male)

Grasshopper warbler

Male blackcap (on right) and female feeding young

Lesser whitethroat

Goldcrests
(female)

Willow warbler

Pied flycatcher (male)

Spotted flycatcher

Grey wagtail

Rock pipit

Goldfinch

Yellow wagtail

Greenfinch (male)

Bullfinch (male)

Linnet (female)

Chaffinch (male)

Yellowhammer (male)

Reed bunting (female)

NUTHATCH *Sitta europaea 14cm*

The subtle grey, buff and chestnut form of the nuthatch, so neatly set off by the stripe of black across the head, is likely to be seen over most of England but becomes rare in the north and west and unknown in Scotland. It is a bird of mature woodland,

Nuthatch

favouring the large branches and main trunks of big oak, beech and other broadleaved trees. Unlike woodpeckers, which prop themselves against a branch using their tails, the nuthatch relies on its light weight, strong grip and sharp claws to keep its footing on bark, and it can happily climb down headfirst or hang beneath a branch using its feet alone.

Its sparrow size, grey upperparts, strong beak and loud, whistling calls (many of them very rapid) make it easy to identify. The nuthatch has a strange habit of taking over a hole in a tree, or a nest box, and plastering all round the entrance with mud until the hole is only just large enough to allow the parent birds access to their nest. It eats insects, berries and seeds, which it will wedge in a crack in bark while it opens them with sharp blows of its bill.

TREECREEPER *Certhia familiaris 13cm*

No bird is more restricted in its outlook on life than the treecreeper, which is destined to spend all its days shuffling upwards, clinging to the bark of a tree, almost mouselike in its movements as it examines every crevice for insects and spiders. As it

reaches the top of a tree trunk or the end of a branch, it will flit down to the bottom of the next, from where it starts again on its upward spiral.

As it goes it often gives a weak-sounding, high-pitched call, but its song, heard from late winter through into summer, is an attractive, whistled phrase ending in a short flourish. It seems almost oblivious to human presence and so can often be seen very closely, when its brown back shows an intricate pattern of buff and white. Underneath it is all silky white.

It has a thin, curved beak and large claws but, though it can cling beneath a branch, usually stays head-upwards, propped up on its stiff tail. The nest of a treecreeper is a small, untidy structure which occupies a gap behind a loose piece of bark.

Treecreeper

GREAT TIT *Parus major 14cm*

Found almost everywhere where there are trees, but generally less commonly than the blue tit, the great tit is easily distinguished by its black head with broad white cheeks, and its yellow underside divided by a broad stripe of blue-black. It has very many different calls, but the strident spring song, based on a metallic 'tea-cher tea-cher' is very obvious.

Though a tiny bird, it is a little bigger and heavier than a blue tit and this is reflected in its life style. It feeds more often on the ground, and on the bigger branches and trunks of trees, whereas the blue tit hangs on the extreme tips of the thinnest twigs with ease. Their respective acrobatic abilities can be compared on the kitchen window peanut feeder in winter.

BLUE TIT *Parus caeruleus 12cm*

Tiny, yellow and green with bright blue on wings, tail and cap, the blue tit is a familiar favourite almost everywhere. It is basically a bird of broadleaved woods, but gardens and parks with plentiful shrubs and trees serve it quite well. In winter it roams more widely, even into reed beds.

Woodland birds generally do better than suburban garden birds in the breeding season, laying more eggs and

Blue tit

rearing more young. This is because the natural habitat is much better for feeding a hungry brood of chicks on the enormous amount of caterpillars needed to nourish them. Like other tits, the blue tit has only one, albeit very large, brood of young each year (up to 14), timed to coincide with the great boom in caterpillar numbers on the fresh leaves of early summer.

LONG-TAILED TIT

Aegithalos caudatus 14cm

Quite separate from the other, true tits, this bird belongs to a different family altogether. Were it not for its lengthy tail, it would be one of Europe's shortest birds. Its tiny size and black, pink and white colours make it unique.

Long-tailed tit

The long-tailed tit is a rare bird at the peanut feeder or bird table. It does not nest in holes, or nest boxes, like the true tits, but builds the most beautiful and intricate nest imaginable. It is an elastic sphere, or ovoid, of moss, lichen and cobweb, with an entrance in the side near the top, hidden away in a thick bush or bramble. Long-tailed tits usually travel in family groups or small flocks, often flying across a road one-by-one in a small stream of tiny, lollipop-like shapes.

COAL TIT *Parus ater 11cm*

Though present in all kinds of woods all over Britain, this bird is best known from conifers, where it feeds high in the needles, making a good view awkward against the light. Its small size (even smaller than a blue tit) helps identify it, and the lack of bright yellow or green can often be noticed. The square patch of white on the back of the neck is its best distinguishing feature.

Coal tit

The song of the coal tit is a strident double note, rather like a great tit's but not so powerful. Otherwise, it has the sharp, high calls common to all the tit family. In winter it will often feed on the ground, looking for beech mast and other seeds. Blue, great, coal and other tits may frequently be found in a single flock. It nests in tiny holes in trees, old walls and even in the ground, which allows it to survive in new conifer plantations which have none of the tree holes needed for nesting by blue tits.

MARSH TIT *Parus palustris 12cm*

Not found in most of Scotland, and unevenly distributed elsewhere, this is never a common bird. It likes old deciduous woods, especially with beech and oak trees. It is very much like a willow tit, but a little cleaner in appearance, paler, with a shiny cap and a neater head. The best identification feature by far is a frequent, loud, high whistle, which sounds like 'pit-chew'.

Marsh tits use small holes in trees for nesting, like blue and great tits. They also eat caterpillars in summer, and seeds and berries in autumn and winter, but are rather rare at bird tables.

WILLOW TIT *Parus montanus 12cm*

Looking extremely similar to the marsh tit, the willow tit is a fraction more heavily built, especially around the head and neck, slightly shorter-tailed, duller on the cap and slightly browner — darker on top and rustier underneath. It does not make a noise like the 'pit-chew' of the marsh tit, but often calls a deep, nasal buzz, like 'nair nair nair'.

Willow tit

Willow tits are found farther north than marsh tits, and are a little more widespread in the south, able to live in bushy hedges and thickets as well as large woods. They also come to bird tables a little more often. Unlike other tits, they make their own nest hole, digging out a cavity in rotten wood — so, despite the name, tend to be found in marshy places more often than the marsh tit!

WREN *Troglodytes troglodytes 10cm*

As short as a goldcrest, but nearly twice as heavy, the wren is one of the tiniest birds of Europe. Its irascible nature, perky habits (especially suddenly appearing from nowhere at the top of a low bush, scolding anyone in sight, then darting off out of view), and rusty-brown colour, with darker bars and a pale stripe over the eye, make it easy to identify. The short, cocked tail is unique. Moreover, if a wren sings in the depths of a still, quiet wood, it is hardly possible to miss it. The voice is astonishingly loud, in a rapid stream of musical warbles and trills.

DIPPER *Cinclus cinclus 18cm*

No bird is more extraordinary than this, a rounded, wren-shaped bird as big as a small thrush, which walks into and under water, even dives in from the air, and swims like a cork on the fastest upland streams. The dipper searches for caddis larvae and other morsels underwater, and nests in a rocky place or a tree trunk actually overhanging a stream. It is tied to its watery environment all year round.

Wren

The male wren makes several 'cock's nests' and attracts a female to look around the choice of property. She will eventually select one, or a new one will be built and used for the eggs. Any of these nests may be used in winter as a place to roost, and on a cold night many wrens will cram in together to keep warm. They will also use nest boxes and up to 60 or more have been counted roosting in one ordinary box! How they all find this one particular box, and why they congregate there after having spent the day foraging alone for insects and spiders, is not known.

Dippers are found all over the north and west of Britain, much less so in the Midlands, and are rare winter visitors in most of the eastern counties. The white bib against a dark body is a unique pattern. Dippers are hard to see against the tumbling waters and rocky edges of a dark stream often lined by old alders and oaks. They give themselves away as they fly, with a loud, unmusical call note — 'zit'.

STARLING *Sturnus vulgaris 21 cm*

A single starling might be taken for a blackbird, as it will often look more or less black, but it has a much more upright, jaunty stance, with its short tail particularly obvious. It walks and runs instead of hopping, and a close view will reveal detailed speckling of cream and lines of brown on the wing feathers that make it unlike any other bird.

Starling at ground nest with its young

Underlying these patterns is a gloss of green and purple, most evident in summer when the pale spots are least extensive. Starlings sit on chimneypots and aerials, waving their wings as they sing a medley of trills, rattles and boyish whistles. In summer they can be found practically anywhere with at least a few trees, from gardens to extensive woods, so long as some open ground — lawns, fields or even the edges of moors — is available for them to search for leatherjackets, worms and grubs. They nest in holes in trees or buildings.

In winter starlings are easy to see and identify because they form large flocks, which gather together each evening into roosts of up to a million or more birds at times — these can be in woods or on the buildings of our larger cities.

BLACKBIRD *Turdus merula 25cm*

Our most familiar thrush, common in gardens everywhere and widespread in woods and farmland, the blackbird is one of Britain's most numerous birds. The male is indeed black, with a broad, rounded tail which it often raises and fans as it lands after a short flight, and a bright-yellow beak. The female, however, is dull, dark brown, and more or less speckled on the pale throat. Her long tail and plodding progress across lawns help identify her.

Blackbirds make solid, basin-like nests of grass, lined with mud and finer grass stems, and raise 3 or 4 broods of chicks each summer. They feed on berries in autumn and winter, but like nothing better than a juicy worm.

The male blackbird has a glorious song, heard best at dawn and dusk — a very rich, fluty sound, with varying phrases each tending to peter out in a scratchy finish. Late each evening, roosting blackbirds set up a loud, almost annoying, chorus of 'pink pink' calls.

Blackbird

MISTLE THRUSH
Turdus viscivorus 26cm

This is our biggest thrush, but tends to be overlooked as it is not a frequent visitor to small gardens. In a large, open garden or park, or on farmland where there are still many trees, it will be more common. It is a pale thrush, particularly when seen, as it often is, raiding the berries of a dark yew tree. Striking white patches beneath the wings are very obvious as it flies (at a greater height than is usual with the song thrush), and it shows pale edges to the tail and pale streaks in the wings. Its breast is evenly covered with broad, rounded black spots.

FIELDFARE *Turdus pilaris 25cm*

In autumn, on the east coast, fieldfares arrive by the thousand from across the North Sea. They eat berries of sea buckthorn and hawthorn, quickly pressing westwards over most of Britain as the crop is depleted, then turning to worms in the meadows. By April they will have returned to the Continent.

Mistle thrush

The usual call is a scolding, dry chatter, almost a hiss, but the song is a fluent, loud and varied performance, with strident and mellow notes intermixed. The 'stormcock', as it is known, will happily sing from a windswept tree-top in the middle of a wet winter's day.

Mistle thrushes are early nesters, laying eggs before the leaves are on the trees, and are very bold in defence of their chicks. They will dive-bomb the local cat, and sometimes its owner too!

While they are here they roam rather aimlessly in flocks, often drawing attention to themselves by their lapwing-like 'wee-ip' calls and harsher, chattering 'chak-ak-ak-ak'. In flight they have white under the wing like a mistle thrush, but on top they show much more contrast, with grey on the head and low down on the back, separated by dark brown, and black on the tail. Close views show a beautiful patterning of black on the face and a deep orange-cream breast, spattered with black.

They often mix with the similar-sized blackbirds, but blackbirds tend to feed in loose groups of maybe half a dozen whereas fieldfares are often in more co-ordinated flocks of up to several hundred at a time.

SONG THRUSH
Turdus philomelos 22cm

This is the classic thrush, the neat, pretty bird of our lawns and parks, though it is also very common in broadleaved woodland. It is soft brown on top, cream beneath with a yellowish chest, all covered with slightly triangular spots of darkest brown. It flies low from the ground into a hedge or bush if disturbed, rarely going over tree-tops like the larger-sized mistle thrush does.

It has one of the most striking bird songs in Britain, a prolonged performance of many short, warbling phrases, each consisting of a few notes repeated 2, 3 or 4 times over. This repetition and the clarity and purity of its voice are its best features.

REDWING *Turdus iliacus 21cm*

Often mixed with fieldfares, the smaller redwing (only starling-sized) is also an autumn visitor, spending that season in our hedges feeding on berries, and the winter and spring in the fields, looking for worms.

It is more like a song thrush to look at, but a little darker, smaller and even slightly lark-like in flight. Under the wing it is a subtle chestnut-red (the upperwings are brown), but the best feature to look for is the pattern of the face. There is a broad dark band through the cheeks, with a stripe of cream above and below; the breast is more streaked than spotted.

Song thrush

On a clear October night it is interesting to stand outside and listen — the soft 'sip' notes of song thrushes and longer, high 'seeep' calls of redwings are commonly heard, showing that the birds are on the move, and winter is on the way. For the redwing's sake, hope that it is a mild one, for few birds suffer so badly in severe weather.

The nest is like a blackbird's but the lining is left as bare, hardened mud. Its eggs are beautifully turquoise-blue with intensely black spots. Song thrushes eat worms but also have a speciality, snails, which are taken to a convenient stone, or 'anvil', and smacked against it until the shell breaks and the soft body is exposed.

REDSTART
Phoenicurus phoenicurus 14cm

The 'start' is this lovely bird's tail, which is continually quivered and fanned to show off its rich orange colour. Males are stunning little birds, only robin-sized, but an eye-catching mixture of black, white, blue-grey and rusty orange. Females are much more subdued, but the tail still shows rusty red.

ROBIN *Erithacus rubecula 14cm*

The friendly, bold robin is a universal favourite — despite the fact that it is an aggressive bird whose territorial disputes may end in death for the loser. Robins are actually rather nasty little birds when in contact with each other!

Only a very young robin, warm brown and spotted with cream, can mislead a beginner, and even then it has a certain perky shape and manner that give it away. Otherwise, all robins, male, female, summer and winter, have the well-

Robin

Redstarts like old woods, with gnarled trees that give them a chance to find a hole in which to nest — but they also take over nest boxes. The best conditions for them are in southern parklands or in the oakwoods of Devon and Wales. The males often choose the very topmost twig of a tall tree as a songpost, and sing a disappointingly brief melody after an optimistic start — usually several fine 'sree sree sree' notes followed by a musical trill or rattle. As with other birds of these woods, many more can be seen once the song is learnt than by relying on sight alone to find them.

Redstarts spend the winter in Africa and arrive here in April. They leave in September, when a few may be seen in the east of England where they rarely nest.

known orange-red breast which is so common (if a little too red) on Christmas cards. Robins are among the most common half-dozen or so birds in Britain, found everywhere where there are trees or bushes. They used to follow wild animals in the woods, looking for worms and beetles where boars and cattle disturbed the ground. Now they do the same with us as we dig the earth in our gardens.

The song of the robin is a little thrush-like, but more wistful, rambling, and less powerful. The bird will nest in a bank, or a hedge, in dense ivy, or in any receptacle that might be thrown into a ditch, like an old tin can or kettle — just part of the adaptability that makes the robin so common.

WHEATEAR *Oenanthe oenanthe 14cm*
Sparrow-sized, upright and lively in appearance, the wheatear is one of the earliest arrivals of all our summer birds. The first ones appear in southern Britain from Africa in early March, and soon move to their nesting areas in the hills of the north and west. In autumn they are more frequent on eastern and southern coasts.

They like grassy places, where they can hop about in short turf. They nest in holes in rocks and stone walls or in rabbit burrows, and eat insects. The best way to identify a wheatear is to wait for it to fly — then it shows a sudden flash of brilliant white over the tail, which has a black tip and centre like an inverted 'T'.

WHINCHAT *Saxicola rubetra 13cm*
Rather like a small wheatear, but much more often perched on a slim stem or a young conifer, the whinchat also comes from Africa in the spring (but not until late April) and nests in the western uplands. It does not have the white rump of the wheatear, but shows small white marks in the tail and wings, and a long, pale stripe

Whinchat (male)

over the eye. Spring males also have a black mask, making them look very handsome. They sing infrequently where they are scarce, but where several males are close together they use song much more, and have a sweet, robin-like warble with a variety of churring notes mixed in.

STONECHAT *Saxicola torquata 13cm*
Unlike the other chats, this bird is with us all year round. In mild winters it can be seen inland and on the coast. If the winter is bad, many die and the bird is restricted to the milder coastal districts, especially in Wales and the south-west, until the population builds up again.

Stonechat (male)

It is a bird of rough, stony ground with gorse and heather, and usually sits up on a prominent perch, or even on an overhead wire. The male has a black head, with a splash of white on the neck and a red chest. Females are browner, but the dark chin and a hint of the same pattern identifies them. They are small, short-tailed, but stockily built birds, sometimes almost robin-like in shape. Their name derives from the call, which resembles stones being tapped together.

NIGHTINGALE

Luscinia megarhynchos 16cm

Famed through the ages for its song, this is a bird that is really very little known to most people. The vast majority of nightingales are found in the south-east and the southern Midlands, where they prefer very dense thickets of blackthorn and coppiced hazel or chestnut. In fact, on bird reserves the best way to encourage nightingales is to revive the ancient practice of coppicing, cutting trees at ground level to stimulate a new growth of dense, slender poles.

The song is, indeed, remarkable, both musical and powerful, with some high, clear notes rarely matched by any other songster, and many phrases that are astonishingly fast. Most characteristic is a slow, rising crescendo of long-drawn, beautiful 'sweeeee sweeeee' sounds often ending abruptly with several deep, full-throated and very quick 'jug jug jug' notes. Nothing else sings quite like this, yet 'nightingales' are often reported in gardens and singing at night at the wrong time of year or in quite unlikely places, and they regularly turn out to be robins singing beside the artificial light of a street lamp! Nightingales are worth going a long way to hear, but the elusive songster usually remains unseen.

With patience, though, it can be glimpsed, hopping about on the ground, looking for grubs. It is a soft-brown bird, rather plain except for a pale ring around each eye and, most conspicuously, a rather bright-reddish tail. It is not so large as is often imagined, being not much bigger than a robin.

GRASSHOPPER WARBLER

Locustella naevia 13cm

This warbler has perhaps the most mysterious voice of all, its song being a continuous trill, a 'reeling' like the metallic ticking of a freewheeling bicycle, which may last for several minutes without a break. As it is best heard near dusk in midsummer, its song by no means implies that you will actually catch a glimpse of this tiny bird.

It is a slim, yellowish-brown warbler, very subtly streaked, but tending to keep well out of sight as it creeps mouselike through tall grass. It is a summer visitor from Africa, reaching Britain in late April and rarely seen after early September. It

Nightingale

likes young conifer plantations, bushy heaths and boggy places, and is found all over Britain though nowhere is the bird at all common.

REED WARBLER

Acrocephalus scirpaceus 13cm
Its name is the best clue to this slim, brown warbler — it lives almost entirely in stands of reed growing from wet marshes, though it will often feed in nearby willows. It has few obvious features, except a rather bright, rusty colour near the tail and a long-faced look. The most distinct characteristic is its song, a low, unhurried, repetitive one with rhythmic, short, churring phrases.

Reed warbler

Reed warblers build nests over water, suspended from vertical reed stems, with a deep cup to keep the eggs safe in a wind. Yet this does not protect them from the cuckoo, which often lays its eggs in these nests. Indeed, the reed warbler is one of the four most frequent hosts for cuckoos in Britain. The cuckoo's eggs are very similar to those of a reed warbler and studies show that, if a very different coloured egg is put in the nest, the warbler will discard it. Why then do they not discard the young cuckoo which soon becomes such a vast and hungry monster? In fact, the cuckoo does not seem to drive the warblers especially hard, as was once thought; its huge gape and shrill cheeping are rewarded by about 15 feeds an hour, which is what the reed warblers would bring to an average family of their own, so they are not overworked by the cuckoo.

Reed warblers migrate from Africa in April but are often not numerous here until May. They return in September, never staying the winter in Britain.

SEDGE WARBLER

Acrocephalus schoenobaenus 13cm
Compared with the reed warbler, this bird is more lively, energetic and easy to see, even singing while flying up out of its reed bed into the open air. It inhabits more varied places, in wet ditches and willow herb or nettle beds as well as reeds. Its song is more excitable, more varied, with scolding chatters mixed with surprising musical whistles.

It looks a shorter bird, with a streaky back and a clean patch of bright buff above the tail. On the head, it has a very obvious stripe of white over each eye. It is also a summer bird in Britain, only here from April to September, but whereas the reed warbler is absent from most western and northern areas, the sedge is much more widely distributed.

Sedge warbler

BLACKCAP *Sylvia atricapilla 14cm*

Sometimes helped by food on bird tables, the blackcap is increasingly spending the winter in Britain, but it is still essentially a summer visitor from the south. It is widespread in woods, liking a thicket of young saplings or rhododendron beneath mature trees.

Males, about as big as a robin, are grey-brown with a small black cap (much smaller than on a marsh tit), but young birds and females are browner with a cap of rusty brown. The male has a superb song, a bright warble that suddenly bursts into a short, powerful phrase that carries well through the woods. Blackcaps eat mainly insects but also a good many berries in autumn, and often ivy berries if they stay the winter.

They are often best seen when feeding on elderberries, or sometimes as they visit gardens to feast on the juicy berries of honeysuckle. A useful way to find them is to listen for their calls, which sound like short, hard taps — usually a single 'tack' every few seconds. This sound is typical of the *Sylvia* warblers (look at their scientific names) while the 'leaf warblers' such as willow warbler and chiffchaff have much softer calls. Compared with the willow warbler the blackcap is also larger and heavier in its movements, is less agile and is not capable of slipping through the foliage quite so smoothly.

GARDEN WARBLER
Sylvia borin 14cm

In many ways a counterpart of the blackcap, the garden warbler is one of the plainest little brown birds of all, without any real marks to break the monotony. It looks a soft, pleasing brown, with a large, dark eye, a faintly greyer neck, and a slightly stubby bill. It is a woodland bird, but is often found in bushier places than the blackcap.

Both have a similar hard 'tack' call note, and the songs can be difficult to tell apart. Normally, that of the garden warbler is a little more prolonged, a little less powerful but more mellow and musical, and without the dramatic change of pace halfway through. Listen for it in the months of May and June.

Garden warblers are not found in winter and are scarce in the north. Despite the name, they are not garden birds.

Garden warbler

LESSER WHITETHROAT
Sylvia curruca 13cm

A little, greyish bird of tall, thick hedges and blackthorn thickets, with a pure-white chin and a rattle for a song — this sums up the lesser whitethroat. It is increasingly frequent but not so common as to be very well known to most people. On top it is dull grey-brown, and it has dark-grey legs. The whitethroat (see next entry) is red-brown on the wings, and has paler legs. Both birds have white sides to their tails, but the whitethroat's looks longer and not as tidy.

Lesser whitethroat

Lesser whitethroats have a quiet warble which turns abruptly into a sound like a child's toy rattle — a dry, quick 'chickachickachicka'. Their 'tack' notes are rather sharper than those made by a blackcap. They are mainly southern and eastern birds, here from April to mid-autumn, and sometimes visit honeysuckle or elder in gardens to take berries.

WHITETHROAT *Sylvia communis 14cm*

This bird likes bushier places and less solid banks of dense thicket than the lesser whitethroat, so it is much more at home in lower, broken hedges and on heaths with plenty of gorse and scattered brambles.

It is a small but long-tailed warbler, with a slightly untidy look despite the rather colourful plumage. The puffy white

Whitethroat (male)

chin and throat always look obvious, but the male's pale-grey head, rusty-brown wings and white-sided tail are more obvious than the female's duller, browner appearance. Whitethroats love to perch low in a tangle of nettles and bramble and scold an intruder with low, buzzing and churring notes, then flit away a few yards to another similar spot, to repeat the performance. They seem nervous, excitable little birds.

The whitethroat has a scratchy, energetic song, often given in a short upward flight from a hedge or wire. This used to be one of the commonest sights and sounds of the countryside in summer until 1969, a year when whitethroat numbers 'crashed'. They have never recovered, due entirely to the continued drought and degradation of the Sahel region, just south of the Sahara. They no longer find food there to sustain them or to build up the fat that fuels their long migration north in spring. The few that do survive still spread themselves over most of Britain, much farther north than the lesser whitethroat.

WOOD WARBLER

Phylloscopus sibilatrix 12cm

Compared with a willow warbler, this bird is a little larger, most noticeable for its longer, often drooped wings. It is greener on top, with stripes of yellow on the edges of its wing feathers, a broad stripe of yellow over each eye and a pale-yellow throat. The underside is purer white.

GOLDCREST *Regulus regulus 9cm*

Europe's tiniest bird, yet tough enough to stay here all year through, the goldcrest is a rounded, dull-green warbler, with wings crossed by bands of dull black and greenish-cream, a plain face except for a smudge of dark at the base of the bill, and

Wood warbler

It is a bird of western oakwoods and southern beeches, both kinds of woodlands which give it space to feed in the tree-tops, looking for caterpillars, and a nesting place among dead leaves in an open area below the trees.

It has a most distinctive song — a short ticking which speeds up into a silvery trill. In fact it also has a second kind of song — a fluty 'pew pew pew'. It often seems to be the case that there are more males than females and some of the most persistent songsters, which sing time after time, hour after hour, are probably males unable to find a mate.

Wood warblers arrive late in April and depart by the end of August and, unlike other warblers, very rarely turn up away from the woods where they nest.

a thin central band on the top of the head. This is usually black with a tiny streak of yellow, but displaying males fan the feathers to show a central patch fiery orange in colour.

Goldcrests like conifer woods above all else, or ornamental conifers in parks, but are really quite widely spread, especially in winter. They are found almost everywhere in suitable habitats.

The song is a test for ageing ears, so high pitched that many people fail to hear it; it has thin, squeaky calls too. The nest of a goldcrest is an exquisite little structure made of cobwebs and moss, slung beneath the tip of a horizontal branch. Inside are the tiniest imaginable eggs, white with spots of pinky-brown.

WILLOW WARBLER

Phylloscopus trochilus 10cm

A song like the musical laughter of tiny children is one old description of the voice of the willow warbler. In early April, when it returns from Africa, there will suddenly be a morning when every tree seems to have its singing bird, giving a sweet, descending cascade of sound over and over again.

A look at the willow warbler will reveal a slender-shaped, greenish bird the size of a blue tit but with a yellower or whiter underside. In autumn, before it leaves, it looks duller, but the young bird is brighter, much yellower beneath, with a clear stripe of yellow over each eye. It is often heard calling a soft 'hoo-eet'. Willow warblers like open woodland, trees in hedges, parks with shrubberies and heaths with scattered bushes. They hide away a grassy nest on the ground and lay tiny eggs, white with red spots.

Willow warblers leave Britain in September, heading further south than the chiffchaff, and it is odd to think that our familiar little warbler spends several months of the year in bushy savanna woodlands, alongside strange sunbirds and barbets, its song heard by lions and elephants rather than rabbits and hares; stranger still that if it survives, it is able to return to the very same spot where it first sang the previous spring, a remarkable feat for such a tiny creature.

CHIFFCHAFF

Phylloscopus collybita 10cm

Another tiny, greenish bird, the chiffchaff looks very nearly identical to the willow warbler. It is a touch duller, clouded with buff beneath, browner above, with a less obvious line over the eye. It has almost black legs — the willow warbler's are pale brown. Easily the best way to tell them apart is by the song. The chiffchaff sings its name, a monotonous repetition of 2 or 3 short, sharp chirps, like 'chiff chiff chaff chep chiff chaff'.

It is more of a woodland bird, less common everywhere than the willow warbler and much scarcer in the north. It makes a domed nest just above the ground in the base of a bush. It arrives here very early, coming only from the Mediterranean area, and may be seen from around mid-March to October.

Chiffchaff

PIED FLYCATCHER
Muscicapa hypoleuca 13cm

Pied flycatchers spend the winter in Africa, reaching their nesting woods in the south-west, Wales and parts of northern England by late April. In spring, but more often in autumn, a few will be seen away from the nesting places, especially on the east coast.

Males are striking little birds, black and white with big white flashes in each wing. Females have a similar pattern, but in dull brown and white. Nevertheless, both sexes are easy to miss in the thick foliage of an oakwood, where they catch flies in midair, or drop to the ground after some tasty morsel. Fortunately, they are extremely fond of nest boxes, and many reserves have high numbers which can easily be watched simply by keeping an eye on an occupied box. Learn the song — a simple, but musical phrase — and you will find many more.

SPOTTED FLYCATCHER
Muscicapa striata 14cm

Much commoner than the pied flycatcher, and found all over Britain, the spotted flycatcher is an eagerly awaited arrival, often not appearing until the end of May. It likes woodland clearings, edges of woods, parkland and shrubberies — a churchyard or tennis court is ideal. Spotted flycatchers often nest in nest boxes as long

Spotted flycatcher

as the boxes have open fronts, not the usual small round hole. They like creepers such as ivy, Virginia creeper or clematis to give the nest some cover.

The bird is basically dull brown, rather pale, with streaky wings and a silvery front. Compared with a garden warbler, it has a much more upright pose and characteristically sits in the open on a post, periodically flying out to catch an insect then returning to the same perch. Behaviour is very much better than plumage colour as a means of identifying the bird.

DUNNOCK *Prunella modularis 15cm*

Dunnocks are quiet, easily missed occupants of most gardens, as well as woods, heaths and even moors all over the country. They are round, dumpy little birds, rather dark, being brown on top

Dunnock

with streaks of black, and grey underneath with streaks of brown. Orange legs give them a touch of colour.

Their song is a flat little warble, the call an insistent, sharp pipe. They make a neat little nest in hedges, and lay clear turquoise-blue eggs. Dunnocks rarely come to bird tables, preferring to shuffle about on the ground, often under a hedge, searching for food such as spiders, grubs and small insects.

MEADOW PIPIT *Anthus pratensis 15cm*
In summer the slim little meadow pipit, streaky olive-brown on top and cream with black lines beneath, is found all over the heaths and moors of Britain, especially on higher ground, but is rare in agricultural districts. In winter it leaves the hills and is commoner near coasts and on lowland fields, where it looks for worms, insects and tiny seeds.

Meadow pipit

It is usually noticed flying up at one's feet, with a longish black tail edged with white and thin, squeaky 'peet peet peet' calls. In summer it flies up from the ground, then flutters back to earth like a tiny parachute or shuttlecock, while giving a thin, trilling song.

On the ground it slips through long grass with ease, looking long and slender, walking instead of hopping as most small birds do. The meadow pipit is often foster parent to the cuckoo and is sometimes seen standing on the back of the monster chick in order to feed the youngster that it has the misfortune to rear!

TREE PIPIT *Anthus trivialis 15cm*
Almost identical to the meadow pipit in appearance, the tree pipit differs chiefly in that it is absent from Britain from late September to mid-April. It is a fractionally heavier bird, more solidly built, less nervous and hesitant in its actions and more confident as it strides over the ground. It tends to be a purer-yellowish colour underneath.

Much more often seen up in a tree, it walks along branches rather than hopping from twig to twig. It calls a buzzing 'teez', quite unlike the meadow pipit's squeak, and its song is much superior, with lovely, musical trills. It sings in a similar 'parachute' flight, but from a twig or high, bare branch, not the ground.

Tree pipit

Tree pipits are quite widespread, though less common in most of Scotland. They like bushy clearings and heaths, young conifer plantations and clearings where trees have been felled.

ROCK PIPIT *Anthus littoralis 16cm*
This bird is like a slightly larger, duller version of the meadow pipit, with a louder call, duller tail edges and much darker legs. It inhabits rocky shores and the tops of sea cliffs in summer, but moves to estuaries and stony beaches in winter, where it often searches for food along the strandline.

GREY WAGTAIL
Motacilla cinerea 18cm

The most elegant and long-tailed of the wagtails, this one is a bird of tumbling streams and mill races in summer, largely confined to the north and west. In winter it is widely spread, even beside small lakes and occasionally on flooded car parks!

It is grey on top, but yellow is the colour that catches the eye — under the tail and on the rump all year and, in summer, bright yellow also on the breast. It has a very sharp, high call note, 'tzip' or 'titik', quite unlike the yellow wagtail, and it has short, pale legs whereas the yellow has spindly black ones.

PIED WAGTAIL *Motacilla alba 17cm*

Males are so black and white that they are unmistakable — sparrow-sized, with long, constantly bobbing tails. Females are duller, grey on top, and young birds greyer still, with only a thin dark mark on the chest and buffish underparts.

It is very common almost everywhere, especially in summer. Waterside places are preferred, but it will nest in woodpiles, old walls, even inside outbuildings if there is a suitable ledge. It is seen feeding on tarmac — footpaths, roadsides and car parks — more than almost any other bird.

Pied wagtail

The two main calls are easily learnt — a whistling 'tchuwee' and a loud, unmusical 'tissick'. The former is an announcement that a bird is holding a feeding or nesting territory, so warning other wagtails to keep away. It may be given in answer to another calling wagtail which is 'knocking on the door', so to speak, to find out if a particular area is already occupied.

YELLOW WAGTAIL
Motacilla flava 16cm

This slim wagtail is a summer visitor, so any wagtail with yellow on from November to March should be a grey wagtail! The yellow wagtail is a greener bird, with longer, blacker legs and a shorter tail. It is not found on boulders in fast streams like the others, but prefers wet meadows, or fields with cattle and horses which scare up a food supply of insects for the bird.

The bird is absent from the north and west and is decreasing almost everywhere. A poor songster, it nevertheless has an easily recognised call, a sweet 'tsweep', usually given in flight which has a distinctly switchback action.

HAWFINCH

Coccothraustes coccothraustes 18cm

Rather bigger and more strongly built than a sparrow, this big-headed finch is nevertheless very hard to spot. In winter it sits very quietly, high up in tall trees, often beech, lime or hornbeam, coming to the ground to feed on fallen seeds only if the coast is clear. In summer it is most difficult

Hawfinch (male)

to see, keeping in the foliage and eating caterpillars, and, later in the season, berries and seeds.

Its calls may give it away, as it tends to fly steeply up into the trees with a sharp ticking note if disturbed from the ground. A glimpse is enough to give the impression of a lot of white, as it has broad patches on the wings and at the tip of the short, broad tail. Close views will show its brown back and otherwise rather pinkish-orange colour, with a black bib, and very thick beak.

Although widely distributed, it is never very common and to most people goes unnoticed.

GREENFINCH *Carduelis chloris 14cm*

In recent years the greenfinch has become more of a suburban bird, but it still prefers tall, ancient hedges, clumps of trees in farmland, and deciduous woods. It is a regular visitor to bird tables and baskets of peanuts, and eagerly strips cotoneasters and other shrubs of their berries. In winter, flocks of up to several hundred roam the fields, feeding on spilled grain and seeds. Whereas flocks of siskins and redpolls fly from tree-top to tree-top in tight parties, and chaffinches live in looser flocks, reacting individually rather than as a unit, greenfinches, like linnets, feed on the ground in tight flocks. These flocks mass together when disturbed, flying up from a field to the nearest hedge and returning together when the source of danger has passed.

It is a stocky finch, about sparrow-sized, with a thick, pale beak. Males are apple-green, females duller and paler, and youngsters browner. All have yellow patches on each wing and each side of the tail, to the greatest extent in the male and the least in the young.

In spring males fly over the nesting area — often a thick yew or tall hawthorn hedge — with a special, slightly butterfly-like flight, wings fully spread and slowly flapping, while singing a series of bell-like trills.

Greenfinch (male)

SISKIN *Carduelis spinus 12cm*
Compared with the greenfinch this is a much more lightly built bird, little bigger than a blue tit, with more contrasts in its colours. Males are green on top, with black and yellow bands across the wings and a black cap and chin. Underneath they are vivid lime-green. Females are paler, much whiter below with black stripes, and greyer on top.

Siskin (male)

GOLDFINCH *Carduelis carduelis 12cm*
The tiny form of the goldfinch seems too small to take so much colour and pattern, but it has black, white and crimson on the head, pale brown and white on the body and black wings with a broad central band of vivid yellow.

They nest in pinewoods of the west (though in the south-west and Wales they are rare) and north, but in winter move over the whole of Britain, often visiting alder trees alongside rivers to feed from the cones, and larch plantations. They move in tight flocks, with quick, bounding flights from tree to tree. When feeding, they are acrobatic, like blue tits.

In spring they are sometimes seen on bags of peanuts — especially red plastic mesh bags. It is suggested that this is the time of year when natural food is most difficult to find, with the previous year's seed crop running low, but quite why the habit has become well established in many areas and not in others, and why red bags are preferred to other colours and types of feeder, is not known.

Goldfinches are not rare, but not really garden birds so they are never very familiar to many people. They prefer thistles in poor farmland, dandelions and sow-thistles that have gone to seed, and teazels on bits of unkempt ground. Some join siskin flocks in alders, or linnets in weedy fields.

The voice of the goldfinch is a very light, liquid twitter, matching the buoyant, airy flight perfectly — not for nothing are the typical small flocks called 'charms'. The song, too, is a rather liquid, flowing performance though with the typical chatter and twitter of a finch. It is usually given from a high perch in a leafy, airy tree such as a poplar or cherry, often in an ornamental avenue or line of roadside trees; modern suburbs with trees and grassy verges are sometimes just the right environment for goldfinches.

LINNET *Carduelis cannabina 14cm*

Once popular cagebirds because of their lively, warbling, canary-like song, linnets are more common than is generally realised. They tend to be overlooked, being so small (much smaller than a sparrow) and often hidden away in tall weeds in some overgrown field. In summer they move out into hawthorn hedges in agricultural land, but much prefer bushy heaths, commons, and strips of land near the coast, where short turf is mixed with gorse and bramble.

Linnet (male)

Linnets are often in small flocks, even in summer, and stop to twitter among themselves at regular intervals. The males are reddish-brown on top and grey on the head. Both the wings and tail are black with white streaks along the feathers. In the spring they have vivid crimson-pink patches on both the chest and forehead.

Females are duller, without the red, much streakier, but still a little greyish about the head and with the white wing streaks. They make a neat, cup-shaped nest of grasses, usually lined with soft, white hair and hidden in a gorse bush or hedge.

REDPOLL *Acanthis flammea 12cm*

One of our smallest birds, the redpoll is a very lightweight finch, with a tiny beak and a deeply forked tail. It is not easy to identify until one learns the hard, metallic rattle which is almost always uttered by a redpoll in flight. A good view, however, will show a rather warm, buffy-brown bird, streaked black, with a yellow bill and tiny black chin patch. A bar of cream crosses each wing. If it can be seen, a little cap of deep red confirms the identity.

In spring, males are much more striking, with the whole underside flushed bright pink. Redpolls are more familiar in winter, especially in birchwoods or larches, often with siskins. They zoom about in close-packed flocks, but can usually be approached very closely with care.

Redpoll

Redpolls now breed over most of Britain, having spread southwards, liking hawthorn bushes on rough commons, young plantations of conifers and the edges of woods. They are occasional in gardens, but do not come to feeders or bird tables.

BULLFINCH *Pyrrhula pyrrhula 15cm*

Beautiful to look at, the bullfinch is detested by fruit growers in the orchards of the south-east and the southern Midlands because of the damage it does to fruit tree buds. It is very selective, ignoring some varieties while completely stripping others.

Normally it will feed on soft buds and, in winter, ash keys. It has a short, thick bill ideally suited to this diet. Males are glorious, blue-grey, black and deep red-pink, with a broad band of pure white around the back of the body. Females are duller, but also have the white, and it is this that is most often seen as a bullfinch or two fly into the depths of a thick hedge. They usually give a low, simple whistle as they go.

Bullfinches rarely mix with other finches and do not join the flocks in fields — they keep themselves to themselves. They rarely sing, and then give only a jerky, squeaky phrase with the reedy quality of a policeman's whistle.

CROSSBILL *Loxia curvirostra 16cm*

So that it can lever the scales from a pine cone, and then insert its tongue to scoop out the seeds, the crossbill has the tip of its bill crossed like a pair of secateurs. Pine, spruce and larch seeds make up its entire diet. It even breeds very early in the year to take advantage of the best of the crop when feeding its young.

Because of this dry food, it is often seen coming to pools to drink, and then it can be very tame. On these occasions, the males show their true colours, a deep red with browner wings and a vivid red rump, which can be hard to see up against the sky. Females are greener, sometimes with a bronzy tinge, and yellow on the rump.

After drinking, or sometimes when they simply decide to move on, crossbills will suddenly fly off a great distance in a strong, undulating flight, giving loud, far-carrying 'chip chip' calls. They are most frequent in the pines of East Anglia, Wales and parts of Scotland, but in some years roam around very widely in search of a good cone crop.

Crossbill (male)

CHAFFINCH *Fringilla coelebs 15cm*

One of Britain's commonest birds, though recently losing ground in the top half-dozen, the chaffinch can live happily in conifer forests (except in the densest stages, when it will only occupy the edge), deciduous woods (where it is most at home), parkland and farmland with trees and gardens with shrubberies.

Chaffinch (female)

It is sparrow-sized and cannot hang from slender stems like a goldfinch or redpoll, or feed from tall grasses like the linnet, but has to content itself with buds, insects and caterpillars in summer and fallen seeds on the ground in winter. It is always very easy to tell, because of the broad bands of white in the wings (though these may be half-hidden when it is perched). Males are quite bright-pink below and, in summer, grey on the head; females are dull, rather olive-grey overall. The song of a chaffinch, given from a perch in a tree, is a short, quick, lively effort, rather rattling and finishing in a fine flourish.

Chaffinches make exquisite nests, neat cups of grass and moss, finished with lichens which camouflage them against the tree trunks, in the forks of which they are usually placed.

In winter chaffinches roam the countryside in flocks, feeding in weedy fields and stubble and on the ground under trees, especially beech. Very often a flock will be all of one sex — the scientific name means 'bachelor', a reference to this separation of the sexes. The males are then browner on the head, but change in spring without actually moulting the feathers. Instead the winter feathers have dull tips, which quickly crumble away in spring, revealing the brighter colours beneath.

BRAMBLING

Fringilla montifringilla 15cm

This is a close relative of the chaffinch, very much alike in shape, pattern and behaviour, but only a winter bird in Britain. Variable numbers arrive in October, to feed with chaffinch flocks in fields and under beech trees. Usually they are rather scarce, but in some years the birds can become quite common over much of England.

Brambling (male)

Bramblings have less white in the wing than chaffinches, much of it replaced by pale orange, but in flight show a broad line of white down the lower back — an instant recognition feature. As with other finches, the female is duller, but the male develops a smart black head and back in spring, set off by a bright, pale bill.

CORN BUNTING

Emberiza calandra 18cm

Curiously patchy in its distribution, the corn bunting is found in cereal-growing areas of the south and east, stretching right up to north-east Scotland, but much more erratically in the west.

It is bigger than a sparrow, more the size of a skylark, but it does not walk about on the ground like a lark and is much more likely to be seen perched on a telephone wire. It feeds on the ground, but moves in short hops like a finch.

The corn bunting is pale brown and cream with dark streaks, with a quite big bill, and has a dry, rustling song like the sound of jingling keys.

Corn bunting

YELLOWHAMMER

Emberiza citrinella 16cm

The pale hen bird, with little yellow, is easily distinguished from a corn bunting or sparrow by the black tail, edged with white, and a rusty-brown rump. The male has these, too, but is usually bright yellow on the head and breast with thin lines of black, which make him unmistakable.

Yellowhammers feed in small flocks in winter fields, and move to bushy places, broken hedges and gorse in the summer. Males sing monotonously all summer through, with a thin, metallic trill usually thought of as 'a little bit of bread and no cheese' — a series of sharp notes with a longer, higher or lower one at the end. The birds are found over most of Britain. The nest is on or near the ground and the eggs are pale with irregular black lines.

REED BUNTING

Emberiza schoeniclus 15cm

With a tail like a yellowhammer's, strikingly white either side, and a basically red-brown back with black streaks, reed buntings should not be confused with sparrows or finches. Females have rather stripy heads, with a hint of red about them, but in spring the males get a jet black head and a broad white collar.

They breed in wet places, all over Britain except for the highest hills and urban centres. Some visit gardens and drier fields, especially in winter, and for a time in recent years they spread to drier habitats for nesting, though this is now less frequent. They are most often found in rushy or reedy marshes and bogs.

HOUSE SPARROW

Passer domesticus 14cm

Very common everywhere, house sparrows need little introduction. Males are always obvious, perky and lively, noisily chirruping all day long, and always with at least some black on the chin. They have a broad red-brown band each side of the head, which is grey on top.

House sparrow (male)

Females are plainer, browner and much less reddish. They are best identified by having pale buffy-grey underparts with no streaks (most finches and buntings have dark lines) and a brown head with a broad, pale line over each eye.

House sparrows live anywhere where people live, feeding on their scraps and nesting in their buildings. A few build large, untidy nests in hedgerows. In the early autumn, large flocks of sparrows, mostly young birds not long out of the nest, gather together in cornfields, and during the winter many will be in mixed flocks with finches and buntings. House sparrows are easy to spot, for there are always plenty about in towns and gardens.

TREE SPARROW

Passer montanus 13cm

This is a far less common bird than the house sparrow, found in parkland and on farms where big, old trees have holes which it can nest in, and in deciduous woods, especially near the edge or in a clearing. In winter, tree sparrows mix with other sparrows and finches in weedy fields, looking for seeds on the ground.

Unlike the house sparrow, both sexes look alike. They resemble the male house sparrow, with a black chin and bright, red-brown back, but the whole of the top of the head is rich brown and, on each white cheek, there is a big, square patch of black.

Tree sparrows are found in odd places (sea cliffs in the west for example) but they are usually less evenly spread than house sparrows and are rather unusual in gardens. Consequently,

Tree sparrow

although they are bright and attractive little birds, they are ignored or overlooked by nearly everyone. Once known, there is one feature that draws attention to them — a call, usually given as a tree sparrow flies by, that sounds like a hard 'tek tek'.

WHERE TO LOOK FOR BIRDS

Birds are everywhere in the British Isles. Even in the centre of cities, starlings and pied wagtails come to roost at night, house sparrows and pigeons make a living among the refuse left by people and kestrels hunt among the sparrows. The variety of birds found in parks and gardens is even greater and town parks provide homes for many species.

You do not have to travel far to see birds, although some very rare species only breed on nature reserves, where they are protected. The classic example of this is **Loch Garten** on Speyside where under the care of the Royal Society for the Protection of Birds breeding ospreys have been protected for 30 years, during which breeding success has enabled them to spread elsewhere in the Highlands until now at least 30 pairs breed in Scotland.

Hides at Cley Marshes

Appropriately the avocet, the symbol of the RSPB, has also spread from the society's Suffolk coastal reserves of **Minsmere** and **Havergate Island** to other sites along the East Anglian and Kentish coasts, including the Norfolk Naturalists' Trust's **Cley Marshes** in north Norfolk and the RSPB's **Elmley** on the Isle of Sheppey.

For the beginner, the great advantage of nature reserves is that information is usually provided. This may be in various

The avocet is the symbol of the RSPB

forms — nature trail guides, information leaflets, displays, or, best of all, communicative wardens. These various interpretational methods give visitors information about what species they may expect to see. On some reserves there may be wardens in the hides who will not only point out interesting species but should also be able to explain how best to identify the birds. There really is no substitute for learning from someone who really knows their birds.

Although the unexpected is one of the joys of bird watching, bird watchers nevertheless need to plan their trips. The birds that you will see will usually be influenced by two main factors — the habitats you visit and the time of year. You will see birds every month of the year, but the greatest variety is to be seen at migrating times in spring and autumn, when the earliest arrivals overlap with the latest leavers. These migrants are most obvious on coasts, but even inland in early April, for example, you might see wheatears on their way north from wintering in Africa to their moorland breeding grounds, and at the same time spot fieldfares, winter visitors about to move north-eastwards to eastern Europe and Scandinavia.

Rutland Water

Waterbirds are the easiest to see and their need for water restricts the places where you might find them. Gravel pits and reservoirs are excellent places to start looking. The best reservoirs are the shallow lowland ones which attract many more birds than the deep upland reservoirs where there is not sufficient vegetation. The use of inland waters for sailing and water skiing does not always mix with bird watching because the birds are disturbed. But on larger areas, such as **Rutland Water** in Leicestershire, **Grafham Water** in Cambridgeshire, **Pitsford Reservoir** in Northamptonshire and **Chew Valley Lake** in Avon, areas have been set aside as nature reserves and wildfowl refuges. Although these places are worth visiting all year round, it is during winter that there are huge flocks of ducks and other waterbirds, but spring and autumn will also produce seabirds on passage and there may be small migrants around the edges. The Wildfowl Trust centres at

Slimbridge in Gloucestershire, **Arundel** in West Sussex, **Welney** in Cambridgeshire, **Martin Mere** in Lancashire and **Washington** in County Durham are all good places to see both wild and captive waterfowl. Again, the best time to visit is in the winter, but there is plenty of interest throughout the year.

Wildfowl Trust, Arundel

Many of the RSPB's 120 reserves are wetlands and some have been created or managed specifically for waterbirds. At **Titchwell** in Norfolk there are both brackish and freshwater pools, attracting birds throughout the year. Hides are provided and it is a very popular place with visitors. To the west is another RSPB reserve at **Snettisham**, less popular with visitors but with dramatic wader roosts of up to 70,000 waders in winter and with nesting terns in summer. The north Norfolk coast is a very good place for birds. **Cley Marshes**, a Norfolk Naturalists' Trust reserve, attracts an impressive list of species and is a mecca for bird watchers. Nearby is **Blakeney Point**, a National Trust reserve for terns, and there is another tern reserve at **Scolt Head**. The **Norfolk Broads** are also well worth visiting. Despite the depressing effects of pollution there are a number of broads that are particularly good for birds.

Estuaries are very good places to look for birds, particularly in winter when wildfowl and waders feed in large flocks on rich food in the inter-tidal mud. The flocks are constantly on the move, feeding on the mud uncovered by the receding tide and moving up the shore as it comes in, eventually moving to high-tide roosts on saltmarshes, rocks and coastal pastures. To see the birds well will depend on the state of the tides and your ability to approach them closely. This means that smaller estuaries, while not so important for large numbers of birds, are actually better for the bird watcher because it will be easier to get in close. At certain weekends in winter the RSPB runs cruises on the **Exe Estuary** to see the wintering avocets and other waders and the views are very good.

A very fine estuary for birds is the **Firth of Forth**. When the tide is out it is a rich feeding ground for waders and when it is in there are large flocks of sea-ducks and, of course, other seabirds.

Dunes on Blakeney Point

The British Isles are very important in world terms for the breeding seabirds. Yet, to many people, seabirds mean only 'seagulls'. Gulls are only a small part of our seabird population. Many of our seabirds spend most of their time at sea, coming ashore only to breed, and then choosing remote islands that are difficult to reach. But not all seabird colonies are remote, and while any bird watcher would find a trip to **Orkney** or **Shetland** very exciting, it is not necessary to leave land. At **Bempton Cliffs** in Humberside there is the only mainland breeding colony of gannets as well as thousands of guillemots, razorbills, puffins, kittiwakes

Puffins

and fulmars. On the other side of Britain in south-west Wales, breeding seabirds can be seen at the RSPB reserve, **South Stack Cliffs**, which are very beautiful in summer and where peregrines and choughs breed. In Scotland, **Fowlsheugh** on the east coast south of Stonehaven is a sensational seabird cliff well worth visiting.

For the more adventurous, boat trips can be taken to the famous gannet colony on the **Bass Rock** in the Firth of Forth or the magnificent **Farne Islands**, which belong to the National Trust and are situated on the coast of Northumberland.

Gannet colony on Bass Rock

Very many birds can be seen in woodland. However, woodland bird watching, though it seems such an obvious way to see birds, can be very difficult. In autumn some of our woods are very quiet, sometimes seemingly almost birdless. Many of the summer visitors have migrated south, and residents are 'recovering' from the long, hard breeding season which drains the energies of adults. They will now be moulting their old, worn feathers, have no need to fight for a territory or attract a mate, and in consequence will be quiet and unobtrusive in behaviour.

Oak, elm and beech forests, a fine habitat for woodland birds

In winter woodlands can be equally quiet, but many birds roam through them in flocks. Once a flock has been located, it is possible to see a lot of birds in a short time — but then the flock will move on.

It is in spring that woods are at their best, with fresh green foliage not yet thick and dark, and birds singing at their best. Places like the **New Forest** and the **Forest of Dean**, the **Wyre Forest** in Worcestershire, the RSPB reserve of **Church Wood**, **Blean** in Kent, **Clumber Park** in Nottinghamshire and many other fine woods are excellent for birds, though few now give much more than a vague idea of what the ancient British 'wildwood' used to be like.

Special birds of the hills and moors are worth seeking in spring and summer, when the weather is fine and before grouse shooting makes the moorlands dangerous in autumn. Moorlands around the RSPB's reserve at **Lake Vyrnwy** in Wales, the **North Yorkshire Moors** and many of the great moors of the eastern **Grampians** have red grouse, merlins, golden plovers and other specialities.

Heather moorland burnt for grouse in the North York Moors

Southern heaths, like **Studland Heath** in Dorset, the reserve nearby at **Arne** and **Thursley Common** in Surrey have other special birds, like Dartford warbler, stonechat, nightjar and hobby in the summer and a chance of a passing bird of prey such as merlin or hen harrier or a great grey shrike in winter.

Farmland habitats are, of course, very widespread, but the traditional idea of English countryside, with buttercup meadows, bushy, overgrown hedges, reedy farm ponds and winding rivers lined with an abundance of flowers such as yellow flag and purple loosestrife, is sadly a thing of the past in most areas. Much of the most varied farmed habitat is found in the south-west — Devon is a rich county — and in the Welsh Marches, where Herefordshire and the old county of Radnor are attractive and full of birds such as buzzards, redstarts, wagtails and flycatchers. Such places are not easily preserved as nature reserves, and those meadows that are protected are almost all reserves for flowers or butterflies — nevertheless, the birds will usually be helped as a consequence.

Many local nature reserves have open days which are worth taking advantage of. Each county has its local Nature Conservation or Wildlife Trust and these very important local organisations maintain nature reserves which vary from tiny areas to large reserves that attract visitors from long distances. You should be able to find details in your local library or through contacting the Royal Society for Nature Conservation.

If it had not been for the efforts of the voluntary conservation movement in this country, many of the places where rare birds breed and many fragile habitats would have disappeared. The organisations listed below will be happy to send details of their reserves as well as membership details.

The Royal Society for the Protection of Birds, *The Lodge, Sandy, Bedfordshire SG19 2DL.*
The Royal Society for Nature Conservation, *The Green, Nettleham, Lincoln LN2 2NR.*
The National Trust, *36 Queen Anne's Gate, London SW1H 9AS.*
The Wildfowl Trust, *Slimbridge, Gloucestershire GL2 7BT.*